THE NEW INQUISITION?

THE
NEW INQUISITION?

*The Case of Edward Schillebeeckx
and Hans Küng*

PETER HEBBLETHWAITE

1817

HARPER & ROW, PUBLISHERS, San Francisco
Cambridge, Hagerstown, Philadelphia, New York,
London, Mexico City, São Paulo, Sydney

FIRST U.S. EDITION

Library of Congress Cataloging in Publication Data

Hebblethwaite, Peter
    The new inquisition?

    Bibliography: p. 168
    Includes index.
    1. Schillebeeckx, Edward Cornelis Florentius Alfons,
1914-   2. Küng, Hans, 1928-   3. John Paul II,
Pope, 1920-   I. Title.
BX4705.S51314H4   1980   230'.2   80-7920
ISBN 0-06-063795-1

---

80 81 82 83 84   10 9 8 7 6 5 4 3 2 1

To my wife,
Margaret

CONTENTS

PREFACE

Saturday 15 December 1979 was a day to remember in the life of the Roman Catholic Church – though theologians may prefer to forget it. In the morning Fr Edward Schillebeeckx O.P. signed the minutes of his meeting with three representatives of the Congregation for the Doctrine of Faith (CDF). They had been investigating his orthodoxy, or strictly speaking the orthodoxy of his book, *Jesus – An Experiment in Christology*. On the same day somewhere else in the same building, Cardinal Franjo Seper, Prefect of the CDF, was signing a declaration which, if acted upon, would effectively put an end to the career of Hans Küng as a Roman Catholic theologian. The day was not done. Just for good measure, that evening at six o'clock Pope John Paul II crossed the Tiber and went to the Gregorian University to deliver an address on the role of theologians in the Church.

A single day, then, that changed the Church, just before Christmas.

Along with the inevitable protests came the questions. Did this presage a new and anti-intellectual phase in the pontificate of Pope John Paul? If Schillebeeckx and Küng could be attacked for unorthodoxy, then who would be next? Was this a return to the methods of the Holy Inquisition? What would the consequences be for academic freedom and the ecumenical movement? Must theologians and pastors always be in conflict?

The New Inquisition? sets out to provide the material for answering these questions. It is as objective as the circumstances permit. It is not written as a pamphlet but as a contribution to contemporary Church history which continues the story begun in *The Runaway Church* and *The Year of Three Popes*.

In order to protect theologians in a 'thorny period' (to use the phrase of one of them), the usual litany of thanks must this time be abbreviated. It will be enough to say that various Dominicans, including most importantly Schillebeeckx himself, gave their full co-operation. But information did not come from one side in the dispute. If the Dutch disdain secrecy, the Romans, despite terrible oaths, seem incapable of it. The book is dedicated to my wife, Margaret, whose christological studies at the Gregorian University proved astonishingly relevant.

Translation was a problem. Where Dutchmen were talking Italian, Italians French and anyone was liable to burst out into German, it was not always easy to recover the original thought. I have done most of the translations myself and aimed at accuracy rather than elegance.

Rome, 25 January 1980   PETER HEBBLETHWAITE

1. *Storm over Schillebeeckx*

In our time faith and theology have become news for the press, and this has led to the development of a *new ethical situation* for the theologian. He can no longer pursue his theological enquiries in detachment from the question of how ordinary people in the Church are going to interpret what he has written.

Edward Schillebeeckx, *The Eucharist*, p. 17

On the evening of 12 December 1979 a sixty-five-year-old visitor arrived at the Dominican headquarters at Santa Sabina in Rome. Bronzed by the sun of the Caribbean, where he had spent two weeks recuperating, he still looked a little dishevelled from travel: the top button of his shirt was undone, his dark blue tie was askew, and his trousers seemed just a little too short. The slightly distrait appearance, the shock of white hair and the black-rimmed glasses all suggested an academic. For the past few weeks radio and television commentators all round the world had been valiantly trying to get his name right: Edward Schillebeeckx. John Whale was not far out in *The Sunday Times* when he suggested Skillabakes as a rough English way of pronouncing it.

Schillebeeckx went into the refectory for supper. Santa Sabina, on the Aventine Hill, has been the mother-house of the Dominicans since Pope Honorius III gave the ancient church to St Dominic in 1219. Though the refectory was redecorated in the baroque style in the sixteenth century, it retains the size and shape it had at the time of Dominic. St Thomas Aquinas ate here.

Schillebeeckx was invited to take his place at the high table. As is the Dominican custom when visitors arrive, he was somewhat redundantly introduced to the community. Such announcements are usually greeted with perfunctory applause. But this time the applause was particularly intense, prolonged and heartfelt, for everyone knew why Schillebeeckx had come to Rome: the next morning he was due to begin his 'conversation' with three theologians (who they were was not then known) at the Congregation for the Doctrine of Faith (CDF). His orthodoxy was suspect. His book, *Jesus – An Experiment in Christology* (Eng. trans. 1979), was under attack. The support of his brother Dominicans – not all of whom agreed with him on every detail – was welcome. But once he entered the CDF he would be alone, armed only with his scholarship and integrity, against the full panoply of a Roman Congregation behind which, dimly perceived, was Pope John Paul II himself. Schillebeeckx had not sought this conflict and did not relish it. He was rather puzzled by the whole business.

He would have much preferred to get on with his scholarly work at the Catholic University of Nijmegen in the Netherlands where he had held the chair of Theology and the History of Theology since 1957. He had celebrated – if that is the right word in the circumstances – his sixty-fifth birthday on 14 November 1979. Normally he would have retired at that age. But because of the likely difficulties of finding a successor – against Vatican rules the Catholic University wanted to be free to consider a married priest for the post – he had been invited to stay on for another five years. He was happy to continue teaching, believing that contact with students kept him alert. But now his work and his teaching were in jeopardy.

His past achievements were considerable. He had written books on Mary, the Eucharist and marriage. Of all his books *Christ the Sacrament* (Eng. trans. Sheed and Ward, 1963) had been the most influential: it may be said to have renewed sacramental theology by presenting the sacraments as a personal encounter with Christ. He had worked as *peritus* or theological adviser at the Second Vatican Council (1962–5) and his hand could be detected in several of the conciliar documents, notably where the Church is spoken of as 'the sacrament or sign of intimate union with God, and of the unity of all mankind' (*On the Church*, No. 1). Later he was the principal theological adviser to the Dutch Bishops and one of the main architects of the Pastoral Council of the Netherlands Province of the Roman Catholic Church from 1966 until 1970, when it was suppressed by Rome. From 1960 to the present he has been one of the editors of the respected *Tijdschrift voor Theologie* (*Review of Theology*), and has helped to edit the multi-language review *Concilium* from its inauguration in 1965. But the CDF was not overawed or impressed by this incessant labour. As early as 1968 it had launched an enquiry into his orthodoxy. At that date the procedure was improvised and in a state of flux. Schillebeeckx did not have to go to Rome himself but was allowed to appoint someone to speak in his defence. He chose Karl Rahner S.J. Rahner convinced the consultors of the CDF of Schillebeeckx's orthodoxy, and the matter was dropped (cf. Richard Auwerda, *Dossier Schillebeeckx. Theoloog in de kerk der conflicten*).

But now in 1979 the interest of the CDF focused on a book first published in Dutch in 1974: *Jezus: het verhaal van een Levende* (*Jesus, The Story of a Life*; the title of the English translation, *Jesus – An Experiment in Christology*, marks a change in emphasis, but I will continue to use it for convenience). If Catholic theologians in the 1960s had been concerned mainly with the nature of the Church and the sacraments – an emphasis that was reflected in the Second Vatican Council – by the 1970s they had moved on to much more fundamental problems of christology. Schillebeeckx was aware of the changing needs. Despite its arduousness, *Jesus – An Experiment in Christology* was a best-seller. The CDF's main accusation against Schillebeeckx, however, was that he did not use the language of the Council of Chalcedon (451) in his account of Jesus. In an interview with Richard Auwerda of *de Volkskrant*, Schillebeeckx explained what he had been trying to do, and said that he was pessimistic about being understood by Roman theologians formed in a different school:

> I tried to help people to grasp how Jesus was experienced by his contemporaries. Jesus shows us what God will be for us and also what man must be for God. I

do not deny that Jesus is God, but want to assert that he is also man, something that has been overlooked. It is precisely as man that he is important for us. But when you say that, you are suspect. They [Roman theologians] always want you to go on repeating the Chalcedonian formulas.

But unless you set the Chalcedonian formulas in the context of Greek philosophy, you will misunderstand them. In my book I tried to make these formulations come alive for the people of today. When you do that, you discover a Christ who puts down the mighty and gives the poor the first place. Yes, that can be revolutionary.   (*de Volkskrant*, 18 October 1979)

Schillebeeckx never subsequently wavered on these points. If theology is, in the phrase of St Augustine, 'faith seeking understanding', then Schillebeeckx's attempt to understand differed from 'Roman theology' only in one respect: he wanted to grasp christology *in its origins* and to show its *historical* setting.

The 18 October interview in *de Volkskrant* went incisively to the heart of the theological debate. But it also acted as a turning-point for public opinion in that it revealed, for the first time, the nature of the enquiry into his theological views. For Schillebeeckx had in good faith accepted the invitation to go to Rome, without fully realizing the form the meeting would take. 'I thought', he explained, 'that it would be an open discussion, a matter of information; but now I understand that a process has been going on in secret and that instead of a discussion there will be a hearing in which I will have to defend myself against certain charges.' There is, it must be admitted, a certain wide-eyed and evangelical *naïveté* about Schillebeeckx. He had to consult a canon lawyer to discover the exact nature of the procedure being used against him (it is discussed more fully in the next chapter). He found it hard to comprehend or to credit the machinations that were being used. He had been invited to a *'colloquium'*. In plain Latin that must mean a 'conversation'; and Roman spokesmen fell over themselves in their anxiety to explain that there was no question of a

14

'trial' or a 'judicial hearing' still less of a 'heresy hunt'. There was a 'procedure'. Nothing more.

The word went out to Vatican diplomats round the world. They were not to comment on the substance of the affair. If asked questions by media people, they were to confine themselves to explaining the 'procedure'. Thus Archbishop Bruno Heim, Apostolic Delegate to England and Wales, was faithfully carrying out his orders when he said that the CDF was concerned with the 'objective impact' of the book, and in no way with the 'intentions of the author' (which no doubt were most honourable). The author would have to 'clarify what he has written so that the faithful are left in no doubt of his fidelity to the doctrine of the Church' (*The Catholic Herald*, 14 December 1979). 'Clarification' was the watchword.

Minds less attuned to such subtleties, however, found it difficult to distinguish between such a doctrinal investigation and a trial. For it certainly resembled a 'trial' in several important respects: a secret investigation had been going on for years, and the author did not know who had made the charges or, at first, what they were; he was to appear before three theologians whose names and competence he did not know; nor did he know – and he never subsequently discovered – who, if anyone, had been appointed to speak in his defence (the *relator pro auctore*); if the judgement on his work turned out to be negative, a 'decision' remarkably like a 'sentence' would follow; and there was no appeal. That such a procedure does not constitute a trial is true only if Humpty Dumpty's principle is accepted: 'When I use a word, it means just what I choose it to mean – neither more nor less' (*Through the Looking-Glass*).

The protests began. They built up throughout October and November. They started in Holland, naturally enough, but they soon became international. I will summarize the main protests in chronological order. Of course, they cannot settle the question of Schillebeeckx's orthodoxy – theological problems are not solved by counting heads. But they are a valuable expression of 'public opinion' in the Church, which even Pope Pius XII held to be legitimate. They will also illustrate how groups of committed Christians responded to the event and tried to decipher its significance. What must have seemed in the eyes of the CDF a relatively simple matter that could be expeditiously dealt with, acquired ever vaster dimensions. The Schillebeeckx 'case' turned into the Schillebeeckx 'affair'. The man became a symbol.

First off the mark were the Reformed (Calvinist) professors of theology from all the Dutch Universities. Their 18 October letter to the CDF drew attention to the harm to ecumenism and the 'serious consequences' for the study of dogmatic theology generally. They recalled how in the pre-conciliar period Catholic and Reformed theologians shunned each other. It was a Reformed maxim that 'Catholics are not to be read'. All that had changed since the Second Vatican Council exhorted Catholic theologians to return to the scriptural foundations of their faith. (They might usefully have quoted here the conciliar decree on Revelation which says that 'the study of the sacred page [i.e. scripture] is, as it were, the soul of theology' – No. 24.) 'Reformed theologians', they said, 'now pay as much attention to Catholic thinkers as to their own theologians; and this is due to the work of Catholic theologians in the Netherlands, among whom Schillebeeckx is the leading figure.' This was an intriguing way of presenting the case: for if one sometimes heard in the Vatican that Schillebeeckx had been unduly influenced by Reformed theology, here were Reformed theologians saying that, on the contrary, they had been influenced by him.

They summarized his achievements, praised his deep knowledge of scripture, his grasp of the Catholic tradition as well as of contemporary philosophy and theology, his creativity and the sheer range of his writings which had brought about 'a new respect for Catholicism'. This did not mean that they had no differences with Schillebeeckx as a Catholic theologian, differences that they had never sought to gloss over. But an inquisitorial procedure could only harm the ecumenical movement and the study of theology. 'We all see our work', they explained, 'as a

16

service to our various Churches, but above all as a service to the truth of Jesus Christ as found in scripture. We have to serve our Churches in the truth, so that the Body of Christ may reach full stature. This service is only possible in freedom ... The man learned in the scriptures is someone who can "bring out of his treasure what is new and what is old" (Matthew 13 : 52).'

By 23 October Schillebeeckx's colleagues in the Catholic University of Nijmegen had bestirred themselves. The entire faculty, including Langdon Gilkey, the visiting professor from the USA, signed a letter written by the Dean of the Faculty, Dr Bas Van Iersel. There were sixty signatures, which gives some inkling of the seriousness of theological studies in Nijmegen. They began by conceding that 'the Church has the right and the duty to watch over the integrity of faith and to sift out new theological formulations. But on the other hand we also hold that it is the duty of theologians to seek to formulate the faith in such a way that it will appeal to our contemporaries.' That was a fair statement of the problem. It distinguished different competencies. Theologians have the duty to be inventive; the *magisterium* has the duty to be vigilant. However, new theological opinions should be discussed first of all among peers. 'It goes without saying', they explained, 'that they must be tested and criticized, but this is particularly the task of other theologians.'

What the Nijmegen Faculty objected to was that this ordinary academic process of challenge and criticism and testing had been short-circuited. The next passage had better be given in full:

We protest as strongly as possible against all procedures which begin with clandestine accusations and in which even the defence remains a secret. We are convinced that such a way of going on contradicts human rights which demand that such procedures should be public and open to inspection, and also that it contradicts the nature and function of theology as a science which presupposes that conflicts between opinions should be the subject of public, scholarly debate; finally, it contradicts the Gospel itself which rejects oppression and servile obedience and calls for freedom. . . .

We consider it a damaging calumny that, for the second time in his life, a colleague of ours should be examined for his orthodoxy, and that it is even possible – as happened in another recent case [i.e. Père Jacques Pohier O.P.] – that he may be punished by being forbidden to lecture or to publish anything without previous censorship. This calumny is in violent contrast with his total commitment to the service of the Church and above all of his mission. That mission is to translate the message and the person of Jesus Christ into a language comprehensible for our time, in fidelity to the intentions of the Gospel, of tradition and of the teaching of the Church.

Similar themes were echoed in the letter to Cardinal Franjo Seper, Prefect of the CDF, from the 'Working Group of Catholic Theologians' of the Netherlands dated 30 October 1979. The new note they added was that the procedure envisaged would 'damage the Catholic Church, hinder its pastoral work and be a set-back to theological studies in our country'. This was a particularly telling argument, since the CDF had been claiming throughout to be acting for *pastoral* reasons: the simple faithful had to be preserved from dangerous opinions. What the 'Working Group' suggested was that more damage was done to the faithful – who are not that simple anyway – by the CDF's action than any of Schillebeeckx's works could possibly have done.

The Catholic University of Louvain which had granted Schillebeeckx an honorary degree in 1974, joined in the fray on 30 October. In a protest signed by professors, lecturers and students, they pointed out that 'Schillebeeckx has for many years worked to show the relevance of the Christian tradition. His entire work is for many a rich store of theological reflection. No one can cast doubt on the scientific quality and the integrity of his work.' They then called for a 'thorough-going overhaul' of the existing procedure and, anticipating the worst, declared that an eventual condemnation of Schillebeeckx or his book would 'pose a threat not only to the academic free-

18

dom of theological research but to the reflection on Christian faith of the Christian community as a whole'. In other words, though the immediate question was theological, it did not concern theologians alone. One sees here the implicit answer to another frequent Roman argument: theologians, it is sometimes said, may advance novel ideas in specialist reviews, but they should not air them in the mass media. But in many countries the distinction no longer holds. The theological genie cannot be popped back into the bottle of specialized reviews.

So far Schillebeeckx had been defended by his fellow theologians. The next group of protests came from those engaged in the pastoral work of the Church, each of whom looked at the Schillebeeckx affair from his own privileged vantage-point, and detected new dangers.

On 9 November the Missionary Council of the Dutch Church addressed a letter to the Papal Nuncio in The Hague. While they recognized that the Holy See had the right to test new theological formulations, they made the by now familiar protest against the secrecy and injustice of the proceedings. 'But our greatest concern', they said, 'is that this process will harm the *credibility* of the Church, do harm to evangelization and to missionary dedication.' As men and women involved in the Church's missionary work throughout the world – and despite everything, the Dutch have continued to provide more missionaries per head of population than any other country – they were particularly sensitive to the need for consistency. They wrote:

> Bishops in South America and in South-East Asia have raised their voices against those who deny suspects an open and fair hearing. The credibility of this message is put in jeopardy when the Church itself, in its own practice, ignores these rights.

The Justice and Peace Commission of the Netherlands discussed the Schillebeeckx affair on 8 November and published a communiqué a week later. Their professional interest led them to concentrate on the infringement of human rights. They were able to quote, with devastating

19

relevance, from the statement of the 1971 Synod on Justice. Chapter 3 is called 'Justice in Practice'. It states the following principles:

While the Church is bound to give witness to justice, she recognizes that anyone who ventures to speak to people about justice must first be just in their eyes. Hence we must undertake an examination of the modes of acting and of the possessions and life style found within the Church herself. (No. 40)

The Church recognizes everyone's right to suitable freedom of expression and thought. This includes the right of everyone to be heard in a spirit of dialogue which preserves a legitimate diversity within the Church. (No. 44)

The form of judicial procedure should give the accused the right to know his accusers and also the right to a proper defence. To be complete, justice should include speed in its procedure. (No. 45)

These clear and admirable principles, the Dutch Justice and Peace Commission concluded, had been flouted in the present case on two grounds: the author did not know who had accused him; nor did he know who was supposed to be defending him. Among the signatories of this statement was Dr Marga Klompe, formerly Minister of Education in the Netherlands and a friend of Cardinal Giovanni Benelli of Florence.

If the Justice and Peace statement was the most hard-hitting, perhaps the most moving protest was that signed by Sr Mediatrix Hoes, President of the Council of Religious, on behalf of the 30,000 religious brothers and sisters of Holland. In their judgement

Fr Schillebeeckx does theology in a way that is shared by many other theologians. It is the sort of theology which tries to bring together, in a synthesis that is both acceptable and thought-provoking, the data of the Bible, of revelation, of tradition and of experience concerning the person of Jesus and his Church. The authors of this letter are convinced that this approach to the mystery of faith is a source of inspiration to many faithful, lay people and religious. In their opinion the writings of Fr Schillebeeckx do not contain 'diverse and strange teachings' (Hebrews 13:9). On the contrary, it is likely that many lay people, clergy and religious, would be truly scandalized if he were to be condemned. They would understand the process by which they believe that Jesus himself was condemned. It was difficult to go further than that: a condemnation of Schillebeeckx would throw light on the condemnation of Jesus. This is not a comparison that Schillebeeckx would ever have made or approved of: that would be a form of megalomania of which he is utterly incapable. But the fact that the official body of religious men and women in Holland could express their feelings so bluntly, so dramatically and – if you will – so clumsily, is part of the record. The Church in the Netherlands as elsewhere depends in so many ways on religious. To alienate them would be an act of folly.

I have left till last the protest of the editorial board of *Concilium*, partly because it is undated and partly because with it we begin to move outside Holland and on to the international scene. Its thirty members represent the cream of international theological talent. First came a whole troop of French Dominicans of every generation (Marie-Dominique Chenu, Yves Congar, Christian Duquoc, Jean-Pierre Jossua, Claude Geffré). Hans Küng and Johann Baptist Metz represented German theology while the Americans Robert Murphy, David Power and David Tracy stood for 'Anglo-Saxon' theology. Gustavo Gutierrez was a third-world witness. (Apologies to the nineteen whose names do not appear here.) Whatever may be thought in Poland, where a campaign of unremitting hostility was waged against *Concilium*, these are not at all wild men or madly aberrant theologians. On the contrary, as the name of their review indicates, they represent an attempt at a permanent and on-going reflection on the consequences of the theology of Vatican II. *Concilium* has sometimes been described as 'the progressive establishment' in the Catholic Church. That may be so: but equal weight should be given to both the adjective and the noun.

The editorial board of *Concilium* declared that Rome could not make a 'unilateral decision' concerning the alleged unorthodoxy of a theologian without taking into account 'the reactions of other theologians as well as of communities, of the public that he addresses, whether restricted or vast, and of his readers'. However, they were not calling into question the existence of a *regula fidei* or rule of faith. But they claimed that in the Church 'there is room for pioneering work which will stimulate the development of a contemporary understanding of Christian faith, in particular with the aid of the human sciences'. In the nature of the case, they suggest, this work will be rather untidy. But theologians should be free 'to do research freely and without being disturbed for some time, and free even to make mistakes which will be put right by the criticism of other theologians'. Abrupt interventions from on high, they say, will be harmful and counter-productive. In any case, disciplinary measures are hardly the best way to help a theologian who may perhaps have strayed from orthodoxy.

The editorial board of *Concilium* is a relatively small group of thirty people. But the *Concilium* secretariat stays in touch with other theologians as possible contributors. In 1968 it had published a plea for liberty in theological research. It was signed by 1360 theologians from all over the world. One may reasonably assume that the original 1360 theologians have not changed their minds; and in the meantime, a new generation of theologians, taught by them, has emerged. So to take on *Concilium* is to challenge a sizeable proportion of Catholic theologians.

The protestors had a practical problem: where were they to send their protests? Some were sent directly to Cardinal Seper, whilst others went to the Papal Nuncio in The Hague for forwarding in the diplomatic bag. In the end a 'national contact address' was provided in Rotterdam, where Fr Ben Vredebregt O.P. endeavoured manfully to keep track of the various initiatives and to co-ordinate them. He sent the originals to the CDF, with copies to the Papal Nuncio in The Hague, to Cardinal Jo Willebrands in Utrecht and to Schillebeeckx himself.

British theologians (the more comprehensive term is used to include the many Scottish professors who signed) had no problem about finding the right address: they wrote a letter to *The Times*, happily restored just in time. It appeared on 3 December 1979. It scotched the notion that the Schillebeeckx affair was of exclusively 'Dutch' interest. Here is the full text:

We understand that Professor Edward Schillebeeckx of the University of Nijmegen has been summoned to Rome by the Congregation for Doctrine (the former Holy Office) to answer certain charges levelled by the Congregation against his writings. We further understand this interview to be the culmination of a quasi-judicial process which the Congregation has been conducting in secret during the last three years, a process in which 'counsel' both for the prosecution and the defence are appointed by the Congregation, 'the counsel for the defence' being forbidden to contact the scholar whom he is appointed to defend.

As Christian theologians (Anglicans, Protestants and Roman Catholics), we acknowledge that any theologian has responsibilities to the tradition in which he stands and whose history and significance he seeks to interpret. We further acknowledge that these responsibilities are distinct from those of the churches' pastors and that as a result the relationship between the theological and pastoral offices will often be marked, as Cardinal Newman noted a hundred years ago, 'by collisions and contrasts'.

Nevertheless, it is incumbent upon both pastors and theologians to exercise their responsibilities in a manner which is consonant with the truth to which they seek to bear witness. We believe that measures such as those currently being employed by the Congregation are inconsistent with fundamental human rights, gravely threaten that freedom of interpretation and research which is an indispensable feature of the human quest for meaning and truth, discredit the authority which employs such measures, and imperil that fragile climate of mutual trust between the churches which had developed in recent decades.

Professor Schillebeeckx's reputation as a man whose scholarship and intellectual integrity are internationally respected will not in the long run be harmed by the procedures to which he is subject. We believe, however, that the damage done to the truthfulness and the credibility of the Christian community is likely to be incalculable. (*The Times*, 3 December 1979)

The letter was evidently prompted by Nicholas Lash, a Roman Catholic who is Norris-Hulse Professor of Divinity in the University of Cambridge. There were eighty-three signatures, a veritable roll-call of theological talent in England and Scotland. Among the Catholics who signed were three Oxford Dominicans, Fr Fergus Kerr, Fr Roger Ruston and Fr Timothy Radcliffe (respectively former Prior, Prior and Sub-prior of Blackfriars), and two Jesuits, Fr John Coventry and Fr Robert Murray. Their names will have been noted in the CDF.

An American petition was organized by Leonard Swidler, Professor of Catholic Thought at Temple University, Philadelphia, and Gerard Sloyan, Professor of New Testament at the same university. It was eventually signed by 120 theologians. A covering letter from Swidler and Sloyan, dated 8 November, makes clear the new factors introduced into the debate by the American theologians. First, they interpreted the Schillebeeckx case as the harbinger of a 'general Vatican backlash against creative Catholic theology'; and, second, they expressed the hope that 'a public counter-move against the secretive, restrictive, condemnatory procedures of the Congregation for the Doctrine of Faith' would 'direct it into more open, dialogic kinds of structures'. In other words they intended their protest to be something more than mere self-expression or impotent lamentation: they wanted it to be effective and to change things. The wording of the petition also represented a novel attack on the problem: it set out to demonstrate that the CDF's procedure contradicted not only Vatican II but Pope John Paul's own statements on the role of theologians:

Whereas, concerning Church renewal and reform, Vatican II stated that 'all are led ... wherever necessary, to undertake with vigour the task of renewal and reform', and that all Catholics' 'primary duty is to make a careful and honest appraisal of whatever needs to be renewed and done in the Catholic household itself' (Decree *On Ecumenism*, No. 4), and,

Whereas, in working for this 'continual reformation of which the Church has always need' (ibid. No. 6), 'the search for truth, however, must be carried out in a manner that is appropriate to the dignity of the human person and his social nature, namely by free enquiry with the help of teaching and instruction, communication and dialogue', and that 'Truth can impose itself on the mind of man only in virtue of its own truth, which wins over the mind with both gentleness and power' (Decree *On Religious Liberty*, Nos. 1–2).

Whereas the present pope, John Paul II, stressed the need he and his fellow bishops and the whole Church have for the work of theologians when he stated that 'The Church needs her theologians, particularly in this time and age ... The Bishops of the Church ... all need your theological work, your dedication and the fruits of your reflection. We desire to listen to you and we are eager to receive the valued assistance of your responsible scholarship' (address at Catholic University of America, Washington, 7 October 1979), and,

Whereas, in the same statement to Catholic theologians and scholars Pope John Paul II respected the need for fostering freedom of investigation when he said, 'We will never tire of insisting on the eminent role of the university ... a place of scientific research' which must apply 'the highest standards of scientific research, constantly updating its methods and working instruments ... in freedom of investigation' (ibid.), and,

Whereas his predecessor, Paul VI, clearly pointed out in great detail that the most apt manner of discerning truth today is dialogue, noting among other things that 'dialogue is demanded by the maturity humanity has reached in this day and age' (*Ecclesiam Suam*, No. 79), and,

Whereas the Vatican Secretariat for Unbelievers, in likewise following this directive, officially stated that 'all Christians should do their best to promote dialogue ... as a duty of fraternal charity suited to our progressive and adult age' (*Humanae Personae Dignitatem*, 28 August 1968, No. 1), and carefully linked dialogue with Church renewal and freedom of investigation when it wrote that, 'The willingness to engage in dialogue is the measure and strength of that general renewal which must be carried out in the Church, which implies a still greater appreciation of liberty ... Doctrinal dialogue should be initiated with courage and sincerity, with the greatest freedom and with reverence' (ibid.).

Therefore we, the undersigned Catholic theologians and religious scholars, wish to express our deep concern about the function and methods of procedure of the Congregation of the Faith, not only in the case of Fr Schillebeeckx, but in general.

In line with the above cited conciliar, papal and Vatican quotations, we believe that the function of any Church leadership *vis-à-vis* theology should not be a negative but a positive one, and that consequently the function of the Congregation for the Doctrine of Faith should be to *promote dialogue* among theologians of varying methodologies and approaches so that the most enlightening, helpful, and authentic expressions of theology could ultimately find acceptance.

Hence we call upon the Congregation for the Doctrine of Faith to eliminate from its procedures 'hearings' and the like, substituting for them dialogues that would be either issue-oriented or, if it is deemed important to focus on the work of a particular theologian, would bring together not only the theologian in question and the consultors of the CDF, but also a world-wide selection of the best pertinent theological scholars of varying methodologies and approaches. These dialogues could well be conducted with the collaboration of the International Theological Commission, the Pontifical Biblical Commission, universities, theological faculties and theological organizations. Thus, the best experts on the issues concerned would work until acceptable resolutions were arrived at. Such a procedure of course is by no means new; it is precisely the procedure utilized at the Second Vatican Council.

Finally, we call on the CDF to turn the December 1979 'hearing' of Professor Schillebeeckx into just such an authentic dialogue, which instead of limiting will liberate all participants for the good of the whole Church.

Certainly, of all the protests, this was the most massive and comprehensive. It may, however, have been a tactical mistake to try to set the Congregation for the Doctrine of Faith against Pope John Paul (who had made other, and less encouraging, remarks about theology in his address at the Catholic University). And we now know that the hope expressed in the final paragraph was forlorn and doomed. Perhaps it never was realistic, if one bears in mind the psychology of the CDF. For it maintains a posture of injured innocence and poses as the martyr of the media. It is not impressed by public opinion and what it considers to be artificially drummed up campaigns. The protests themselves become further evidence of how far the theological gangrene has gone, and therefore of the need for rapid surgical intervention. I owe this metaphor to a 'Vatican source'.

The 'internationalization' of the case made it clear how far Schillebeeckx was now playing a largely symbolic role. For neither the letter to *The Times* nor the Temple University petition made any mention of christology, which was the original point at issue. Instead, they broadened the scope of the debate to include academic freedom, the relationship between theologians and the *magisterium* (or the pastoral office of the Church), the spirit and methods by which theological conflicts should be resolved and, finally, the worrying direction taken by the pontificate of John Paul II. One issue can unlock all issues.

It is true that most of these themes had at least been adumbrated in the Dutch protests, which had a far more 'popular' base. But the Dutch had very properly concentrated on the 'injustice' of the procedure, and they interpreted it in the light of what they saw as a continuous pattern of attacks on their Church since the end of the Council: the 'corrections' made to the *New Catechism* (popularly known as the Dutch Catechism); the winding up of the Dutch Pastoral Council in 1970; the imposition of two conservative bishops – Adriaan Simonis in Rotterdam and Jan Gijsen in Roermond; and – finally – the Special Synod of the Dutch Church which was due to meet in Rome in January 1980. Their reasoning was that since Schillebeeckx had been involved in all the progressive developments of the Dutch Church, an attack on him was also an attack on them. Schillebeeckx himself admitted that there was no 'objective connection' between his 'hearing' and the Dutch Synod; but he also recognized that it was impossible to prevent people in Holland from establishing such a link.

In Dutch eyes, the hearing meant that the whole postconciliar Church was on trial; on the international level, it meant that post-conciliar theology was on trial. And all agreed that justice was being flouted. Such was the gravity and importance of the case. The over-worked word 'crisis' was, this time, wholly appropriate.

One last protest deserves a special mention. On the three Sundays before the hearing, a group of theological students from the University of Amsterdam stood outside church doors to collect signatures for their petition. It brought together many of the themes already discussed. Here are its main points:

E. Schillebeeckx has a central place in modern Dutch theology. He has constantly tried to make the authentic Catholic tradition comprehensible so that it could become the inspiration of faithful pastoral practice.

E. Schillebeeckx was for many years an adviser of the Dutch Bishops, and he played an outstanding part in the Second Vatican Council and in the Dutch Pastoral Council ...

This shows that an attack on Schillebeeckx does not merely affect him personally; it is an attack on theological studies in the Netherlands and it creates an obstacle to the positive developments of the Dutch Catholic Church.

We believe
– that conflicts which develop between Holland and the central administrative organs in Rome should be discussed openly and in complete sincerity,
– that the present conflict could be solved by holding a properly Christian dialogue instead of the present one-sided procedure.

The Amsterdam students collected over 60,000 signatures, brought them personally to Rome – where most of them had never been before – and had immense difficulties in delivering their petition. The 'proper channels' were the Dutch Ambassador to the Holy See; but he was reluctant to be involved in so contentious an issue. After much anxious telephoning, Cardinal Agostino Casaroli's secretary told them to hand in their petition at the Portone di Bronzo on the right of the Vatican. They took their three-foot-high package past the Swiss Guard and left it in the office. No one quite knows what happened to the petition thereafter or where the 60,000 signatures, some smudged by rain, are now filed.

Schillebeeckx, the man at the centre of the storm, was unaware of many of these developments. On 21 November he had collapsed while lecturing at Nijmegen. A cardiac specialist said that it was not a heart attack. But he advised complete rest. On Saturday 24 November Schillebeeckx set off for an undisclosed Caribbean island, where he remained until he went to Rome on 12 December. By then, he knew that he had plenty of support in Holland and from theologians all over the world. But none of this was particularly relevant when he arrived at the Congregation for the Doctrine of Faith at 8.30 a.m. on the morning of 13 December. He had been asked to come early so as to meet Cardinal Seper before the hearing proper began at 9.30. He obeyed. The road to Rome had been a long one. It was just over six years since he had written in the Foreword to *Jesus – An Experiment in Christology*: 'It is for the reader to judge whether this approach is successful or not; and on that score reasoned criticism of any sort is most welcome' (7 October 1973). Among his more attentive readers had been the experts of the CDF. They initiated the procedure which brought him to the dark and gloomy courtyard of the Congregation on 13 December 1979.

How that procedure was applied, and what its legal basis is, will be the subject of the next chapter.

2. 'Not a Trial, but a Clarification'

Nowadays, the Church prefers to make use of the medicine of mercy rather than of severity. She considers that she meets the needs of the present by demonstrating the validity of her teaching rather than by condemnations.

Pope John XXIII, opening speech at Vatican II

Most Catholics, having better things to do, are cheerfully ignorant of the workings of the Roman Curia. Theologians do not pay it much attention either, except when it forces its attentions on them. It is mostly bishops and religious superiors who have to bear the immediate brunt of its decisions, and then have to try to communicate them to the uncomprehending faithful.

The Curia is commonly described as 'the Vatican bureaucracy'. This description fits in a general way. It is at the service of the reigning pope. In theory it carries out what he decides. Of course, it does not always work out just like that: forces of inertia may prevail, entrenched interests may prove hard to shift, and the Curia can become, instead of the 'servant' of the Church, a 'power' in its own right. The late Cardinal Giacomo Lercaro believed that this happened in the pontificate of Pope John XXIII, with the result that he suffered from 'institutional solitude'. But he bypassed and outwitted the Curia by summoning the Second Vatican Council.

The various traditional departments of the Curia are known as Congregations (they would be 'ministries' in a secular government). They deal with different sectors of the Church's life – with the appointment of bishops, the clergy, Catholic education, evangelization (missions) and the like. In the post-conciliar period these traditional Congregations have been 'balanced' by the setting up of new bodies such as the three Secretariats (for Christian

31

Unity, non-Christian Religions and Unbelievers) and, more feebly, by Commissions (such as that for the mass media, euphemistically called 'the means of social communication') and Councils. The bureaucracy has expanded. It was truly said that a problem was not acknowledged to exist in post-conciliar Rome unless a body had been created to deal with it. There was an evident rivalry between the 'old' Curia and the 'new' Curia. They represented different interests and different mentalities. The Secretariat for Christian Unity, for example, frequently found itself at loggerheads with the Congregation for the Doctrine of Faith. Without loss of integrity, it was concerned with flexibility in doctrinal statements, while the CDF continued to defend orthodoxy conceived in the narrowest way. Under Paul VI, an uneasy balance was on the whole maintained. Under John Paul II, it seems that the balance of contrasting forces no longer exists. It was the CDF that acted against Schillebeeckx.

The CDF had always claimed a pre-eminent place among the Roman Congregations. It was not concerned with this or that activity in the Church but with doctrine itself. It could therefore intervene anywhere where doctrine was threatened. For this reason it had been known, when it was the Holy Office, as the *supreme* Congregation. Its supremacy had been greatly whittled away in the last fifteen years, but it had a long tradition of repressiveness and intolerance which was difficult to live down and hard to abandon. Founded in 1542 by Pope Paul III in order to combat heresy as the Reformation was getting under way, it was at first known as the Congregation of the Inquisition and later as the Holy Office. Its original building can still be seen in Piazza Minerva, just opposite the elephant. Its most famous victim was Galileo. It was attacked in the most vigorous terms for its defensiveness and hostility to theological research, by Cardinal Joseph Frings of Cologne at the Second Vatican Council on 10 November 1963.

There was widespread agreement that the Holy Office was in need of reform. Even its Prefect, the redoubtable Cardinal Alfredo Ottaviani, *bête noire* of the progressives at the Council, agreed that change was needed. Indeed, he claimed that it had already happened. He said in 1966: 'The procedure has been changed ... The accused has a greater chance to defend himself, to express his own opinion and have it discussed. We have returned to the procedure envisaged by Benedict XIV. We have to admit that in the course of centuries the Holy Office had departed from that procedure and substituted an authoritarian approach. It was unfortunate that this happened' (Interview in *La Gente*, 13 April 1966). Since Benedict XIV had reigned from 1740 to 1758, one may say that it had taken an unconscionably long time to implement the procedure so wisely 'envisaged' in the age of Enlightenment. It is not for nothing that 'We think in centuries here' is a favourite Roman maxim.

Paul VI clearly intended to complete the unfinished business left by his eighteenth-century predecessor. He had witnessed the harm the Holy Office had done in the 1950s to theologians like Yves-Marie Congar O.P. and Henri de Lubac S.J., who later became experts at the Council. He wanted a change of heart at the Holy Office. On 7 December 1965, the crowded last-but-one day of the Council, he published his *motu proprio* or binding decree, *Integrae Servandae*, by which the name of the Holy Office was changed to that of the Congregation for the Doctrine of Faith. It was intended to be far more than a mere change of name. I well remember the day. 'Flashed it round the world', said the then Reuters' bureau chief in Rome, 'it's the end of the 'oly inquisition. No more thumbscrews. You have to simplify a bit.' Paul VI put it rather less picturesquely than John Organ did, but his meaning was substantially the same. The Congregation for the Doctrine of Faith was to have not merely a watchdog function but the positive task of encouraging and promoting theological endeavour. He quoted 1 John 4:18 which says that charity excludes fear and said that 'the best way to defend the faith is to encourage sound doctrine'. This might, of course, involve 'fraternally correcting errors'. But that was not the main point. Paul VI wrote:

33

One cannot and should not ignore the progress of human culture, which is important in religious matters, and it implies that the faithful will follow with greater adhesion and love what the Church teaches if they can see with greater clarity the reasons for definitions and laws, in so far as this is possible in matters of faith and morals.

We may translate: heresy hunts in secret were to cease; the CDF would have to justify its positions and could not merely rely, as in the past, upon 'higher authority'; dialogue would replace juridical procedures. The whole concern for sound doctrine would become more evangelical.

The CDF in its new incarnation had been told the direction in which it was to move. But it had not yet been given new regulations (a *regolamento* or *ratio agendi*). And without a *ratio agendi* it was lost. For the juridical spirit had not been banished by the mere force of papal exhortation. The apostolic constitution, *Regimini Ecclesiae Universae* (15 August 1967) which was concerned with the overall reform of the Roman Curia, promised a new set of rules for the CDF. They took a long time to come. In the meantime, Schillebeeckx had his first brush with the CDF and emerged unscathed, thanks to Karl Rahner's resourceful advocacy. It was not until 15 January 1971 that Paul VI, at a meeting with Cardinal Franjo Seper, Prefect of the CDF, formally approved the *Nova agendi ratio in doctrinarum examine* – the new procedure for examining doctrinal problems.

Since this *ratio agendi* is little known and since it will no doubt govern future procedures, it will be useful to go through it now and set down the successive stages which led, eventually, to Schillebeeckx's appearance in the first-floor room of the CDF on 13 December 1979. (The Latin text is *Acta Apostolicae Sedis*, 1971, pp. 234–6.) Each point will be accompanied by a brief commentary, in which first the official interpretation of the text is given (based on the commentary in *Osservatore Romano*, January 1971 and the 'inspired' article in *La Libre Belgique* of 30

November 1979), and then the application to the Schillebeeckx case, if known, will be explained.

1) *Books or articles which have been drawn to the attention of the CDF are submitted to the weekly meeting – it happens on Saturdays – of the Congregation. If they contain 'clearly and certainly an error in faith and if the publication of such an opinion would do harm to the faithful', they may ask the Ordinary or Ordinaries to inform the author and invite him to correct the error.*

It would be interesting to know precisely how a process begins. It is not altogether clear. We know that anonymous denunciations are not accepted. They must be signed, serious and solid.

In fact it is impossible to say who launched the procedure against Schillebeeckx, though he had been attacked, with monotonous regularity, by right-wing publications in Holland, notably the review *Confrontatie*. But that in itself would not have been enough to take action. Otherwise the workload of the CDF would soon become intolerable.

The option of inviting the Ordinary to speak with the incriminated theologian was not followed in the case of Schillebeeckx. (Rather confusingly, this is called the 'extraordinary' procedure.) There was, in any event, an ambiguity about 'Ordinary or Ordinaries' that would bedevil the whole case: since Schillebeeckx was a Dominican, a religious, his Ordinary was the Master General of the Dominicans, Fr Vincent de Couenongle; but since he was also teaching in the Catholic University of Nijmegen, one could also consider the Chancellor of the University, who happened also to be the President of the Episcopal Conference, and the Archbishop of Utrecht, as the appropriate Ordinary. The CDF opted to consider the Archbishop of Utrecht as the Ordinary, but only after Cardinal Bernard Alfrink had resigned and been replaced by Cardinal Jo Willebrands. The significance of this is that Alfrink had always defended Schillebeeckx, and made him the principal theological adviser of the Dutch

Bishops. *Jesus – An Experiment in Christology* is dedicated to him. It was he who told students: 'Read the Bible – and then Schillebeeckx.' What Willebrands thought was not at that time known.

It is a moot point whether the Master General of the Dominicans, de Couenongle, as a co-equal 'Ordinary', ought to have been involved. He was in fact kept in the dark and on 12 October 1979 wrote to an understandably aggrieved Dutch Dominican Provincial: 'I know practically nothing of this matter. I have received only two letters. Their content was inadequate.' CDF canon lawyers extricate themselves from this difficulty by claiming that 'Ordinary or Ordinaries' means one or the other and not both.

But the most remarkable feature at the start of the process is that the author is already presumed to be guilty of 'error'.

2) *The Congregation has to decide whether a more detailed study is required in order to discover whether the controverted opinion is in harmony with 'divine revelation and the* Magisterium *of the Church'.*

Note the equivalence – somewhat hasty, to say the least – between these two terms. For although the *Magisterium* or teaching authority covers only what is contained in 'the deposit of faith' as it is spelled out in the course of time, in practice it has come to mean whatever has been taught by previous councils and popes. This is the phenomenon known as 'creeping infallibility': it tends to overflow its strict limits and to invade every corner of Church life and doctrine. Thus on most theological questions there is a division between 'maximalists', who seek to broaden the scope of the *Magisterium*, and 'minimalists', who try to keep it within proper bounds. The 'minimalists' are no less loyal to the *Magisterium* and, in the long run, a lot more useful to it.

In the case of Schillebeeckx the Congregation decided that a more detailed study was indeed required. Two 'experts' were therefore appointed, together with the 'spokesman for the author' (*relator pro auctore*) whose role is explained in the next section. The very definition of roles seems to pre-judge the case: for if someone is appointed to defend the author, it must be presumed that the other two are going to attack him. So it is not so much a matter of 'discovering whether' the author's opinion contradicts 'divine revelation and the *Magisterium*' as of 'showing how' it contradicts them. And at this stage the author knows nothing of what is going on behind closed doors.

3) *The two assessors present their report to the CDF; and the man appointed to speak 'for the author' does the same. His task is 'in a spirit of truth to indicate the merits and positive doctrinal aspects of the author's work; to help to reach the true meaning of the author's opinions in theological context and to interpret them correctly; to answer the questions put by the assessors and the consultors; and to give his assessment of the influence of the author's opinions'.*

That sounds fair and innocent enough.

But in fact this part of the procedure could act against the interests of the author. His spokesman has to 'answer the questions put by the assessors': but in this way they are alerted to the likely strategies of defence. He has to ensure that they 'interpret the author correctly': but this saves them from presenting too caricatural a picture of the author's views. However favourable to the author the spokesman for the defence may be – whether out of genuine conviction or as a 'let's suppose' intellectual exercise – he contributes to a dress rehearsal for the eventual *colloquium* and participates in a 'dry run', a dummy trial. His judgement on the influence of the author is also a double-edged weapon, for there would be no need to proceed against an uninfluential and unread author. Schillebeeckx's spokesman could hardly plausibly claim that he was uninfluential; but in this topsy-turvy world the result would be that the need to act against him was even greater. The main function of the *relator pro auctore* is to permit secrecy to be maintained, for he, like all the participants, is bound by 'the pontifical secret'.

For that reason we do not know who Schillebeeckx's assessors were. It is a reasonable inference – though by no means certain – that those who took part in the hearing had previously given their opinion; and that would point to Fr Jean Galot S.J. and Fr Albert Patfoort O.P. Both are Rome-based, can read Dutch, and have an interest in christological questions. There is not an endless supply of theologians who meet the specifications. But the identity of Schillebeeckx's 'spokesman for the defence' remains a mystery. There are indications that it was Fr Valentine Waldgrave, a Dutch Dominican who had written careful studies on John Henry Newman. By an interesting quirk of fortune and the accident of the alphabet, his name can be seen alongside that of Karol Wojtyla in the end of term reports at the Angelicum University for the year 1948. Waldgrave is a member of the International Theological Commission. At their October 1979 meeting he is said to have expressed his disquiet about the Schillebeeckx affair to Cardinal Seper, who replied with a vague, dismissive gesture. If Waldgrave was the mysterious 'third man', the defence spokesman, his participation was limited, and it was later alleged that his report in favour of Schillebeeckx had been used against him.

4) *The experts and the spokesman for the author present their reports to the Council of the Congregation. All the relevant documents in the case are distributed to the Cardinals of the Congregation, at least a week before they are due to consider the matter.*

One might observe that this is a very second- or third-hand way of going on. In the case of Schillebeeckx the cardinals were invited to read reports about a book written in another language which was of considerable length (727 pages in the English edition). Just conceivably they might already have read it, but that cannot be guaranteed: cardinals are busy men. To have to read a summary of complicated historical arguments does not seem the best way to get to know the mind of the author. His ideas, developed in a context of faith, are reduced to a set of 'opinions' which can be juridically examined. The dominant concern is to lay bare errors and ambiguities. This was admitted by Mgr Carlo Molari, President of the Italian Theological Association. He holds the unique distinction of having been once employed by the CDF and also having been a victim of it. He knows both sides. He said that Cardinal Ottaviani had once remarked: 'It is just as well that the Epistles of St Paul were not submitted to the Holy Office for scrutiny. He would not have been able to meet our stern requirements of clarity and absence of ambiguity.'

5) *The Cardinals of the CDF meet. The Prefect presides, introduces the discussion, and gives his own opinion on the matter in hand. The others then give their verdict in order of precedence and a vote is taken.*

From what subsequently happened, we may deduce that this meeting took place early in 1977. Cardinal Seper presided. Of the remaining nine cardinals who had the right to be present (it does not follow that they actually were), two are now dead: Cardinals Villot and Wright. The others were: Cardinals Baggio, Angelo Rossi, Garrone, Willebrands, Baum, Felici, and Schröffer. They will re-appear later in our story. Clearly the majority vote must have been against Schillebeeckx, otherwise the case would have proceeded no further. From now on Willebrands knew what was happening. He was involved from two points of view: as a member of the Council of the CDF and as Schillebeeckx's 'Ordinary'.

6) *Either the Prefect or the Secretary seeks an audience with the Holy Father, presents him with the complete dossier, and puts to him their suggestions for further action.*

The Prefect of the CDF was (and remains) Cardinal Franjo Seper; the Secretary was (and remains) Archbishop Jérôme Hamer O.P. Their recommendation was that Schillebeeckx should be invited to provide 'clarifications' in writing on the disputed points. Paul VI approved. This decision was communicated to Schillebeeckx via Cardinal Willebrands. The letter from Seper to Willebrands was dated 13 April 1977, and had the protocol number 46/66.

Schillebeeckx then wrote the twenty-two page reply which is given in Appendix 1.

7) *If the author's written reply is found to be unsatisfactory, he may be invited to have a conversation* (colloquium) *with those appointed by the CDF.*

Schillebeeckx's lengthy reply clearly failed to satisfy the CDF. We know this because in a letter dated 6 July 1978, October of that year was proposed as a suitable time for a 'conversation'. But the death, first of Paul VI on 6 August and then of John Paul I on 29 September, seemed to relieve Schillebeeckx of his obligation to make himself available. The Curia, apprehensive about its own future, was preoccupied with other matters. Schillebeeckx dropped out of view.

Since one of the reforms of Paul VI was that all prefects and secretaries of Roman Congregations had to tender their resignations on the death of a pope – a sensible provision designed to give the new pope a free hand – it might have seemed that Schillebeeckx was let off the hook. (I recall a French Jesuit Provincial who, faced with an imposing pile of dossiers from his predecessor, instructed his secretary to 'burn them'.) But this was a faulty appreciation.

However, the date of Schillebeeckx's original summons to Rome makes it clear that Paul VI had been involved, however reluctantly. So the argument of the CDF was to some extent valid: one cannot say that the Schillebeeckx hearing *in itself* is proof positive that the pontificate of John Paul II would be more energetic in the repression of theological thinking. On the other hand there is some evidence that in his last months Paul VI was weary of life and not completely in control of what his subordinates were doing. The dynamic 'co-ordinator', Giovanni Benelli, had gone to Florence as Cardinal, and his replacement as *sostituto*, Giovanni Caprio, was out of his depth. And certainly one may say that the CDF, under John Paul II, has felt stimulated in its task of denouncing errors.

So we reach 13 December 1979. The *ratio agendi* had been followed, though not too scrupulously: its weakest point, juridically, was that the Master General of the Dominicans had not been kept properly informed; and one could quibble over the propriety of continuing under one pontificate a process that had been started under another. But since there were no precedents for the application of the new rules, it was difficult to determine the exact legal position. But the CDF case was strong enough to summon Schillebeeckx to Rome a second time. The conversation could take place.

But with public opinion outraged and Schillebeeckx overnight a folk-hero of contemporary Catholicism – often among those who had never opened any book of his, still less the daunting tome that was allegedly under discussion – the CDF had to react publicly. But how could it communicate? The Vatican Press Office was more than usually useless. Since it had never admitted that anything was happening, it could hardly venture to comment on a non-event. And since, in any case, its denials and *mises au point* are commonly found to be incredible, it was a blunt and useless instrument. So Archbishop Hamer did the only thing possible in such a dire situation: he used the old-boy network and made use of F.D., initials which conceal a Brussels parish priest who also doubles up as Belgian correspondent for *Osservatore Romano* and can be relied upon to say whatever he is asked to say. The hope was that his article in *La Libre Belgique*, a Brussels daily, would be picked up elsewhere. Of course one cannot prove that the 30 November article signed F.D. in *La Libre Belgique* was directly inspired by Hamer; but it puts the CDF case well and photocopies of it were distributed by Hamer to friends and well-wishers in Rome.

The centre-piece of the CDF argument was an outright denial of the idea that 'human rights' or their infringement had anything to do with the case. True, theological writers do have certain rights: they have the right not to be travestied or misunderstood. Hence the talk of 'clarification': the question is – did you really mean that? But this 'right' is qualified and set in the context of 'the right of the faithful to receive sound and authentic doctrine'. If one has in advance decided that the author is purveying unsound and unorthodox doctrine (and without such an assumption, a case could not even start), then clearly the author's rights have to give way to the (numerically) superior rights of the faithful. The claims of 'academic freedom' are subordinate to the claims of 'pastoral need'. But there is to be no 'heresy hunt' and – above all – no 'trial'.

This theme was later developed in the press statement issued by the CDF – for the first time in its history – on 13 December 1979. 'The questions are formulated', it explained, 'so as to arrive at a clarification, and they are far removed from any polemical intention.' *La Libre Belgique* had already anticipated this position, by a remarkable coincidence: 'There is no question of a "trial" but rather of a pastoral conversation.' The only question at issue – and it is a profoundly 'pastoral' question – is whether 'these propositions are, yes or no, compatible with the faith of the Church.' 'The purpose of the meeting', concludes F. D. Hamer, 'is not to refute the author or to impose a retractation on him.' The author is free to say what he likes. He is not asked to withdraw anything. All he has to do is answer the questions and sign the minutes of the meeting as a faithful record. His partners in dialogue do not have to decide anything: the decision is left to a subsequent meeting of the Cardinals of the Congregation.

That sounds bland and innocuous enough. But it overlooks one of the principal features of this friendly pastoral conversation: the interlocutors, who must on no account be called 'judges' or 'jury' or 'prosecution', represent 'authority' in the Church, whereas the theologian represents only himself and his painfully elaborated ideas. The scales are not even. Appropriate action depends on the judgement of the three theologians appointed by the CDF. And what 'appropriate action' is no one knows until it has been taken. Here the article in *La Libre Belgique* becomes almost touching in its pseudo-*naïveté*.

For it coolly states that since the *ratio agendi* does not say what should or might happen to the incriminated theologian, the only reliable course is to look to precedent. And the only precedent offered is the rather discouraging one of the French Dominican Jacques Pohier who, because of his book, *Quand je dis Dieu,* had been forbidden to lecture, or to say Mass, in public. He may continue to teach, but only in private; and he may continue to write, but only subject to the most stringent conditions of censorship. If that was meant to encourage Schillebeeckx on the eve of his visit to Rome, it hardly seemed likely to achieve its purpose. The fact is that a procedure that has no clear sanctions, indeed no specific sanctions at all, delivers those who fall foul of it into the realm of the arbitrary. 'The Sacred Congregation will decide the matter' is all it has to say. So one will only know what it *may* decide, after the decision has been reached. And there is no appeal.

Schillebeeckx submitted to the procedure of the CDF, though he was far from happy about it. He made this clear at his press conference after the hearing. 'But', he said, 'I am a Catholic Christian and I accept the judgement of the *Magisterium* in matters of faith ... I felt obliged in conscience to come to Rome, while deploring the infringement of human rights involved in the procedure. The complaint was not merely that the first stage of the investigation should have been completed without informing or consulting me. At an early stage someone must have made up his mind that there were errors or heresies or ambiguities in my writings. I was only brought in at a later stage.'

Schillebeeckx added, however, that the word 'heresy' had never been pronounced, and that the formula most commonly used was that he should 'clear up ambiguities'. But he did not think that the method adopted by the CDF was well suited to this end. For the real differences between himself and the representatives of the CDF were not on this or that proposition: they were differences of method and approach – and different propositions appeared only at the end of a long process, and could not be understood unless the long process itself had been first unravelled.

So before presenting the conversation between Schillebeeckx and the interlocutors appointed by the CDF, we shall have to tackle their contrasting approaches to christology. This will involve an excursion into the deep hinterland of theology: but without such a journey, the essential point at issue in the Schillebeeckx case will go by default.

3. *Dialogue of the Deaf*

When orthodoxy comes in by one door, charity goes out by the other.

Fr Martin D'Arcy S.J., in 1951

What was it about *Jesus – An Experiment in Christology* that had so upset the Congregation for the Doctrine of Faith? The most obvious place to look for an answer was the list of nine topics or questions proposed to Schillebeeckx for discussion in his colloquy with the Roman theologians. They were: 1) the nature of divine revelation; 2) the normative value of ecumenical councils and the importance of the papal *magisterium*; 3) Jesus Christ as Son of God and pre-existent Word; 4) the sacrificial value of the death of Jesus; 5) Jesus' awareness of being Messiah and Son of God; 6) Jesus and the foundation of the Church; 7) Jesus and the institution of the Eucharist; 8) the virginal conception of Jesus; 9) the 'objective reality' of the resurrection. It was a pretty stiff examination by any standards, and it would have to be concluded in about eight hours. It made a doctoral examination look like child's play.

A comparison of Schillebeeckx's book with this agenda brings to light a rather surprising fact: he had simply not dealt with about half of these themes in *Jesus – An Experiment in Christology*. He had not formally discussed 1), 2), the second part of 3), and nowhere had he dealt at any length with 8). This suggested that he was being reproached not so much for what he had written as for what he had not written. It was a line of defence that he sometimes tried: his book on Jesus was a prelude (of 727 pages!), an opening up of the field, and in no way was it presented as a complete and finalized christology. He promised later work on the christology of John and Paul, not dealt with in this book, which was confined to the

45

Synoptic gospels. But this very incompleteness and tentativeness were turned against him. He ought to have known better, said Fr Jean Galot S.J., Professor at the Gregorian University. These questions were all settled fifteen centuries ago at the Council of Chalcedon in 451. There was no point in raking over the ashes of past controversies: one would merely find new versions of old heresies.

At this point one becomes aware of a contrast of theological styles so striking that there seems little hope of understanding between them. Yet Schillebeeckx and Galot had a lot in common. They were both Belgian, though Schillebeeckx was Flemish-speaking while Galot was a Walloon. Schillebeeckx was five years older than Galot, who was born on 31 August 1919. Yet this comparable background resulted in very different attitudes. It is not enough to contrast them as Dominican and Jesuit: for many Dominicans are less enlightened and learned than Schillebeeckx, and many Jesuits are more receptive to new ideas than Galot. The difference between them can be put this way. For Galot, there may be the appearance of open discussion of a problem, but in the end, when the crunch comes (and it comes fairly swiftly), the answers are already given in the Councils of the Church. The answers are, so to speak, at the back of the book: you may not look at them whilst working out your problem, but then you consult the back of the book to make sure that you were right. Schillebeeckx's method is quite different. When he asks a question – say, about the meaning of the title 'Son of God' – he sets off on a genuine investigation. He does not know in advance what the answer will be; and nothing can tell him in advance what the answer ought to be. Councils may and do provide interpretations of this title, but they cannot *determine* what it meant in the context of the New Testament: that can only be discovered by inspecting the texts themselves. Of course Schillebeeckx knows perfectly well that one can never return to a state of 'original innocence' *vis-à-vis* the scriptural evidence. We cannot pretend not

46

to know the answers given by tradition. But methodologically they are secondary.

What I have called contrasting 'styles' Schillebeeckx himself calls, more accurately, 'models', and he points out that there will be a transitional period in which conflict is only to be expected:

> For a while old and new culture models will co-exist; the respective champions of the two models often come into conflict; there is even polarization at times: two groups of people, though contemporaries, live in mutually 'alien' worlds, they cease to understand each other.... That in the process of rethinking the faith mistakes will be made goes without saying – how could it be otherwise? But these are the humanly unavoidable by-products of what are authentically Christian attempts to prevent the faith from becoming an historical relic and to make it a living reality, here and now.... Those who (for whatever reasons) fail to understand what is going on will – true to that apocalyptic model – utter their reproaches; for they have a fixed impression that faith is being – the charitable among them would say involuntarily, but others systematically – eaten away from within.... I do not begrudge any believer the right to describe and live out his belief in accordance with the old models of experience, culture and ideas. But this attitude isolates the Church's faith from any future and divests it of any real missionary power to carry conviction with contemporaries for whom the Gospel is – here and now – intended.

(*Jesus – An Experiment in Christology*, pp. 581–2) Schillebeeckx here predicted exactly what would happen, and the reasons for it. This passage is essential for understanding his project: he is neither arrogant nor swashbuckling, he does not sound like a heresiarch, and his sole concern is to restore saving power to the Gospel. But since theologians with different habits of mind cannot grasp this, there will be only a *dialogue des sourds*, a dialogue of the deaf.

Theological misunderstandings arise when theologians

47

argue from different premises. Raymond E. Brown has usefully analysed the range of differences on christology, the question at issue in the Schillebeeckx case. (*'Whom do men say that I am?'* – *a Survey of Modern Scholarship on Gospel Christology*, in *Biblical Reflections on Crises Facing the Church*, 1975, pp. 20–37). First he distinguishes 'non-scholarly conservatism' from 'non-scholarly liberalism'. 'Non-scholarly conservatism' (which prevailed in the Church as a result of the reaction to the Modernist crisis in the early years of this century) refuses to admit that there is any significant christological *development* within the New Testament. If Jesus enthusiastically endorses Peter's confession of faith in Matthew 16:16, then that is the way Jesus thought and spoke; and this truth is not undermined by the fact that Jesus' reaction in Mark is quite different, nor by the fact that in Matthew 16:23 Jesus calls Peter 'Satan'. Again, if John speaks of Jesus as a pre-existent divine figure (cf. 8:58; 17:5), then this reflects Jesus' own self-understanding, even though the Synoptics do not present him in this way.

'Non-scholarly liberalism' reacts against 'non-scholarly conservatism', or may even be a consequence of it. The discovery that the gospels are not a stenographic record of Jesus' sayings and doings leads some to throw everything overboard. The statement that 'christological development occurred' leads to the anxious questions: 'But how do I know when to stop?' and 'How do I know what to believe?' 'Non-scholarly conservatism' had everything neatly docketed and tied down; 'non-scholarly liberalism' has thrown everything into the melting-pot.

There are 'scholarly' versions of both these attitudes ('scholarly' in the sense that the ground has been personally worked over and the results published in reputable biblical journals). Thus 'scholarly liberalism' is sceptical about arriving at the historical Jesus of Nazareth, but reasonably confident that it can make statements about the faith of the early Christian communities who responded to Jesus. It places christological development *within* the experience of these primitive communities. The merit of 'scholarly liberalism' is that it was sensitive to the highly varied nature of the milieux in which the Gospel message was received, developed and handed on. It makes us aware that there were different theological viewpoints. Thus titles which in one context might seem to indicate divinity (like 'Lord' and 'Son of God') do not do so universally.

'Scholarly conservatism' accepts the historical method of 'scholarly liberalism' but rejects its sceptical value judgement: it believes that it is possible to push back beyond the faith of the early Christian communities to the historical Jesus and his ministry. Thus a link is established between the historical Jesus and the Christ of the Easter faith. The Christian message becomes more coherent – and more reliable. But at this point there is a division between those who hold that the christology of Jesus was *explicit*, and made use of titles such as 'Lord', 'Son of God' and 'Prophet', and those who hold that it was largely *implicit* so that Jesus conveyed the sense of who he was not by using (or accepting) particular titles but by 'speaking with unique authority and acting with unique power' (op. cit., p. 34). Schillebeeckx holds the second view.

This is a very brief summary of a long debate. Its purpose is to make one thing clear. On this analysis, Schillebeeckx appears as a 'scholarly conservative' who leaves Bultmann and his school of 'scholarly liberalism' away to his far left. And Galot appears – at least as far as New Testament studies go – as a 'non-scholarly conservative'. That judgement may seem a little harsh on someone who is, after all, a professor at the Gregorian University. But all those Catholics who did their scripture studies before 1964 are likely to have been taught by 'non-scholarly conservatives'. In 1964 the Pontifical Biblical Commission published an 'Instruction' on *The Historical Truth of the Gospels*. It distinguished three stages in the formation of the gospel tradition. In stage one the limitations in Jesus' presentation of himself are recognized. Stage two concedes that the christological faith of the early Church was post-resurrectional in origin (this leaving room for 'form-criticism'). And finally the Instruction acknowledges that the gospels are written in the light of different situations (thus leaving room for 'redaction-criticism' or consideration of the 'editorial' role of the evangelists). Schillebeeckx worked within these parameters and exploited them. Some of his critics do not appear to have heard of their existence.

The suggestion that Schillebeeckx is a 'scholarly conservative' may seem a little far-fetched: but there is enough room to the right of Bultmann to accommodate him. In the rest of this chapter I shall show how his historical method helps to resolve some of the problems posed by the Council of Chalcedon. Then, in a final section, we shall see Fr Galot heroically and Canute-like trying to stem the tide of non-Chalcedonian christologies. The melancholy conclusion will be that though a Schillebeeckx is capable of comprehending a Galot, without approving of him, a Galot can neither comprehend nor approve a Schillebeeckx.

Schillebeeckx's method is above all *historical*, in several senses of this elusive term. It means first of all and most humbly that he will examine the data in chronological order, in so far as that is discoverable. This has an immediate consequence for New Testament studies. It means that one will discover several layers of strata in the text (the metaphor is borrowed from geology). Not everything in the material that comes down to us was written at the same time. The most likely view is that the Passion narratives came first (as their length and extensive detail suggest), and that these were filled out with post-resurrection stories and accounts of Jesus' ministry; finally, at a later stage, came the 'birth of Jesus' stories found in Matthew and Luke. To point out these obvious facts (their working out is of course far from obvious) is not to tear the heart out of the New Testament: it is to make it more intelligible as a human document. 'Look at the process as well as the result', advised Lord Acton. It is the condition of understanding. Schillebeeckx looks at the process or genesis of christology.

The second sense of 'historical', as used by Schillebeeckx, is a little more difficult to grasp. Historical may be contrasted with 'mythical' and both have to be distinguished from what is 'of faith'. To illustrate this one cannot do better than quote from the traditional creed which mingles together, indiscriminately, matters of history, myth and faith. For example:

Christ was conceived by the Holy Ghost,	1)
born of the Virgin Mary,	2)
suffered under Pontius Pilate,	3)
was crucified, dead and buried;	4)
he descended into hell;	5)
he rose again from the dead:	6)
he ascended into heaven.	7)

Statements 3), 4) and half of 2) are historical in the sense of having been, at one time, empirically verifiable; and enough evidence perdures for us to accept their validity today. There was somebody called Jesus, whose mother was Mary, who was crucified while Pontius Pilate was governor of Palestine. Thus he died and was buried. Thereafter we move into trickier realms. The clearest affirmation of faith is that 'he rose again from the dead'. The remaining remarks could be construed as 'mythological', provided one remembers that 'mythological' does not mean false. On this point one may consult James P. Mackey, *Jesus, the Man and the Myth,* who observes that to call this or that 'mythical' does not tell us whether the New Testament is right or wrong, but rather 'how to read what it has to say' (SCM, 1979, p. 82). For myths – that is, images or stories with significance – can attach themselves as much to real persons as to fabulous figures. In our example of the creed, for example, it is possible to discuss whether item 5) ('he descended into hell') has the same value as item 1) ('he was conceived by the Holy Ghost'). Certainly this 'hell' is not the place of later theology, from which there is no escape: inevitably, then, a process of demythologization begins in which the *point* of this statement rather than what it literally asserts is what matters.

To make these distinctions is not the same as making outright denials. As we shall see later, Schillebeeckx was forced into corners where his interlocutors gaily mingled the three distinct areas, and all Schillebeeckx could say was: 'But that is a purely historical question.' This happened, for instance, in the discussion on the empty tomb, for so long considered as evidence of the truth of the resurrection. Schillebeeckx pointed out, with total unoriginality, than an 'empty tomb' proves nothing one way or the other – there could have been various ways of explaining why the tomb was empty which fell short of resurrection; and in any case – and this is the important point – faith in the resurrection does not and cannot *depend on* the historical fact, if it is a fact, of the empty tomb. It is based rather on the evidence of lives that have been·turned upside-down by the power of the Spirit of Jesus.

Schillebeeckx's approach is historical in a third sense. He takes things as they come. Thus he rejects the Galot method of starting from the Council of Chalcedon and then reading the New Testament through the spectacles of Chalcedon: the only result of that will be eye-strain and consequent headaches. For the fully developed christology of Chalcedon – which happened, it should be remembered, more than four centuries after the events it interprets, and therefore chronologically stands in relation to the death of Jesus as we stand to the reign of Queen Elizabeth I – cannot be used as the sole key to the interpretation of the New Testament. That would be an anachronism which Schillebeeckx wishes to avoid. This is not to say that Chalcedon was wildly wrong or was not a legitimate development of New Testament data. Catholic Christians who accept the wisdom of ecumenical Councils and consider them to be a legitimate development, are nevertheless not bound to regard them as having said the last word or, necessarily, the most relevant word for the late twentieth century. It would indeed be remarkable if concepts hammered out in the light of available Greek philosophy in 451 should prove to be equally enlightening fifteen centuries later. Remarkable and, on the face of it, somewhat improbable.

Schillebeeckx, as already noted, did not deal with these questions at any length in his book, though he was forced to pay attention to them in subsequent discussion. His position is that too literal fidelity to Chalcedon would be the greatest infidelity of all, since the language used by Chalcedon had a precise philosophic meaning which is no longer current today. Consequently, one is 'faithful to Chalcedon' not by repeating what it said, but by trying to say in different language 'what it intended'.

To illustrate that these positions have nothing outrageous or startling about them, I want to refer to a book written by Gerald O'Collins, an Australian Jesuit teaching at the Gregorian University: *What are they Saying about Jesus?* (1977). He gives five reasons why Chalcedonian christology poses problems. First, it is a christology 'from above'. Its initial question is 'How does the pre-existent Word enter our world?' But this starting-point makes it difficult to grasp the true and developing humanity of Jesus. True, he looks like a baby and cries like a baby; true, he is crucified in a most horrible way. But underneath it all he is divine, and so the reality of his human experiences is made suspect.

Secondly, in the christology 'from above', the central mystery of Christian faith becomes, of necessity, the *incarnation* itself. Prayer contemplates in deep wonder the marvel of the God-made-man. There is nothing wrong with that, except that it changes the New Testament emphasis on the Passion and Resurrection. The birth of Jesus is at the centre of the story, and what happens after Christmas becomes the unfolding of a plan worked out in advance, in which it is difficult to speak of 'development' or 'growth'. The definition of Chalcedon concentrated on the incarnation, and so switched the attention away from the *saving* Passion and Resurrection. This is not to say (with Don Cupitt) that faith in the incarnation should be abandoned: what is being suggested is that it should not be emphasized at the expense of the work of redemption.

A third consequence of starting from the formulation of Chalcedon is that it commits us to endless and unfruitful wrestling with insoluble philosophical problems. How can we unpack the statement that Jesus is 'true God and true man' without sacrificing one element to the other? There is a sort of theological algebra implied in the attempt to put together 'two natures' into 'one person'. The 'two natures' doctrine can easily give the impression that Christ is divided into two layers, that he is a double being with two juxtaposed natures. As O'Collins remarks, '"One person in two natures" sounds almost like a man with two jobs or someone with dual nationality' (op. cit., p. 7). So this terminology obscures the difference between being human and being divine. Equal difficulties cluster round the term 'person'. For Chalcedon has traditionally been taken to mean that Jesus may be called a divine person but not a human person: he is a divine person who assumed human nature. But to the contemporary mind, to deny human personhood is to deny humanity. There are no such things as 'human natures' floating about in a disembodied way waiting for a person to take them over.

The fourth weakness of traditional christology is one it shares with the creeds: they make an astonishing leap from 'born of the Virgin Mary' to 'suffered under Pontius Pilate'. The whole ministry of Jesus has been left out. His preaching, his miracles, his healing activity – all this has been by-passed. Now this might be satisfactory enough for a Bultmann, who does not believe that the historical Jesus could be recovered and does not think that this matters either way. The 'Christ of faith' was enough for him. Schillebeeckx reacts against these omissions. He devotes an important section of his book to the ministry of Jesus (Part II, pp. 105–271). Hans Küng, likewise, in *On Being A Christian* (1977), makes the discussion of the ministry of Jesus the centre of his book.

Finally, traditional christology concentrated the attention on the person of Jesus rather than on his saving work. It asked who he was rather than what he did. Treatises lavished space on his divine-human constitution, but neglected the fact that the titles he is given in the New Testament – and not only that of 'Saviour' – express different aspects of his work of salvation and correspond to the aspirations towards salvation that were current among his contemporaries. In other words, the ontology of Jesus (the study of his essential being) had come to replace a functional approach (concerned with what he did) and soteriology (concerned with his saving action). The ancient creeds, of course, do not overlook that Christ's coming was 'for us men and for our salvation' (*propter nos et propter nostram salutem*), but subsequent christology had not given this insight the attention it deserved.

In *Jesus – An Experiment in Christology* Schillebeeckx returns to the sources and attempts to put back together again what later theology had separated. Part III (pp. 399–571) is devoted to the response to Jesus crucified and risen. He explores what salvation meant for Jesus' contemporaries. As expectations varied, so too did attempts to formulate Jesus' role as 'Saviour'. He could be seen as 'the Lord of the Future', as in Mark's christology, or as 'the Son of God', or the starting-point could be 'Wisdom' literature or the 'Easter-experience' itself. Each of these 'models' adds something to our understanding of the impact made by Jesus on his contemporaries. At the end of this long Part III, Schillebeeckx makes a remark which sums up what I have been saying all along and permits one to grasp what he was trying to do:

From the Council of Nicaea onwards one particular christological model – the Johannine – has been developed as a norm within very narrow limits and in one direction; and in fact only this tradition has made history in the Christian Churches. For that reason the course of history has never done justice to the possibilities inherent in the synoptic model; its peculiar dynamic was checked and halted and the model relegated to the 'forgotten truths' of Christianity. Although our own time is not connected therefore with this or that pre-Nicene Christology by means of a continuous tradition, nevertheless there are factors present in our experience of cultural and social life which put pertinent questions to the Nicene Christology and its historical dominance, and so open up perspective offering a view of possibilities before Nicaea. (pp. 570–1)

One would have thought that the experts of the CDF

55

ought to have appreciated and valued this project. For Schillebeeckx's aim is not so much to subvert Chalcedonian christology as to enrich and supplement it with earlier and more scriptural 'images' of Jesus, who is the Saviour. Far from 'undermining Christian faith', one can say that his work contributes greatly to its strengthening since it helps to make intelligible what would otherwise be intolerably puzzling. And even if one is not prepared to go so far, then at least it may be allowed that the best way to test the hypotheses of Schillebeeckx is to subject them to reasoned and public academic debate. To turn the discussion into a 'loyalty test' and an examination of 'orthodoxy', or even in the end a matter of 'discipline', is surely the worst possible way to arrive at the truth. When theologians become, not colleagues engaged in a common search for a better way of understanding the mystery of Christ, but accusers and inquisitors, then a grave disservice is done to the cause of truth.

Fr Jean Galot had entered the lists as accuser and inquisitor long before he faced Schillebeeckx across the table in the CDF on 13 December 1979. To say that he had 'pre-judged' the issue would be a profound understatement. To prove this one does not have to rely on the hearsay evidence of his students at the Gregorian University, who report that his lectures consist for the most part of a sustained attack on all theologians who have departed, or whom he believes to have departed, from the sound doctrine of Chalcedon. His most recent book, *Cristo Contestato* (1979), proves that these reports are well-founded. The first part of the book is a polemical account of 'non-Chalcedonian christologies'. Schillebeeckx is summarized in seven pages (and no attention is paid to *methodological* questions), Küng in six pages and, among the other nine theologians attended to, one notes the names of two Americans (David Tracy in *The Blessed Rage for Order*, New York, 1975 and Monika K. Hellwig who contributed the christological section to *An American Catholic Catechism*, Seabury Press, New York, 1975). Galot's book is a useful guide to possible future operations of the CDF. Since he believes that non-Chalcedonian christologies are in error, all he is required to prove is that he is dealing with non-Chalcedonian christologies. And since most of his authors admit this, the demonstration is not very difficult.

No attention is paid to methodology or to the 'horizon' out of which the new christologies appear. But if he is short on method, Galot is long on motives. He thinks he knows why these theologians have gone astray:

> The fundamental intention of non-Chalcedonian christologies is anthropological. Their concern is to adapt themselves to contemporary man. This leads them to 'humanize' the message of revelation, to give it dimensions more adapted to the man who has to receive it. The mutability of dogmatic expressions and the relativistic approach to the formulations of faith not only justify the transposition of dogmas into contemporary language, but also their translation into more human and more 'horizontal' language.... Traditional faith in Jesus is reduced to the exemplary faith of Jesus. There is also a tendency to see in Jesus the revelation of what man is, rather than a revelation of God, though the latter is not excluded ...
>
> (*Christo Contestato*, pp. 102–3).

What is distressing about this approach is that here Galot lumps together indiscriminately a dozen theologians, does not distinguish between them, and conducts a *procès de tendance* on all of them. The most extreme statements are taken as the norm. Thus Jacques Pohier O.P., already condemned by the CDF in April 1979, is alleged by Galot so much to want to make Jesus an 'ordinary human person' that he denies that Christians ought to seek consolation in his cross (in *Quand je dis Dieu*, pp. 173–81). This contrasts with the sober pages of Schillebeeckx. Nor is Galot's accusation of an 'anthropological' intent quite so devastating as he seems to think. The emphasis on what revelation means for man is something that is found in the Second Vatican Council, notably in a text that is a favourite quotation of John Paul II: 'Christ the Lord, Christ the final Adam, by the revelation of the mystery of the Father, *fully reveals man to man himself* and makes his supreme calling clear' (*Church in the World of Today*, No. 22; my italics). To bring out this aspect of revelation is an essential task for theology today. What Galot hastily calls 'relativism', the theologians he attacks would want to call 'relevance'.

If we were dealing with an informed and open theological debate, it would be perfectly possible for the roles to be reversed and for Schillebeeckx to be addressing searching questions to Galot. He could enquire, for example, whether Galot is completely happy with the formulations of Chalcedon, and raise the objections found earlier in this chapter. He could ask whether mere repetition is enough to secure relevance for contemporary man. And so on. The contest would be equal, the procedure open-handed, the outcome illuminating. However, we are not dealing with an informed theological debate but with an action of authority. And so the questions come from only one side. They are put by Galot with an insensitivity to what Schillebeeckx was trying to do such that one feels it would have been better if he had been excluded, or voluntarily withdrawn, from the entire exercise. Galot's thin juridical cover is the oft-repeated statement that the CDF was not concerned with 'the subjective intentions of the author' but only with 'the objective impact' of the book.

Even if we accept, provisionally, this rather shaky distinction between 'intention' and 'fruits', Schillebeeckx does not come out too badly. The evidence gathered in chapter 1 does not suggest that he has undermined anyone's faith. Rather the contrary. The religious of Holland noted that his 'approach to the mystery of faith is a source of inspiration to many faithful, lay people and religious'. One reason for this, I suggest, is that Schillebeeckx thinks of theology not as a set of abstractions but as *a story about salvation*. His *Jesus – An Experiment in Christology*, is framed by two significant *stories*.

The first is found in Acts where we read of a cripple who is daily carried to the gate called Beautiful. Peter healed him and then addressed the Jewish authorities who had become concerned about the affair: 'Be it known

58

to you all, and to all the people of Israel, that by the name of Jesus Christ of Nazareth, whom you crucified, whom God raised from the dead, by him this man is standing before you well ... *And there is salvation in no one else'* (Acts 4: 10, 12). The New Testament is not a theory or a philosophical treatise: it is a story of salvation that involves us, ineluctably.

Despite its daunting technicity, Schillebeeckx's book itself tries to keep to the form of a story about salvation. It is narrative theology. That is why Schillebeeckx ends his book with a story recounted by Martin Buber about an old rabbi:

> My grandfather was paralysed. One day he was asked to talk about his teacher – the great Baalschem. He related how the saintly Baalschem used to leap about and dance while he was at his prayers. As he went on with the story, my grandfather stood up; he was so carried away that he had to show how the master had done it, and started to dance and caper about. That is how stories should be told. (p. 674)

And that is how Schillebeeckx tries to tell 'the story of a life' (his Dutch title). Telling the New Testament story transforms both the hearer and the narrator. But it is difficult to put that into neat syllogisms.

4. *Roman Colloquy*

They had no conversation properly speaking. They
made use of the spoken word in much the same way
as the guard of a train makes use of his flags or his
lantern.

Samuel Beckett, *Waiting for Godot*

Even apart from its historical associations, the palace
which houses the Congregation for the Doctrine of Faith
is a dispiriting place. Its five storeys are just on the left
of St Peter's Square, beyond Bernini's colonnade, and its
address, 11 Piazza del Sant'Uffizio, recalls its old name,
which is still preferred on the Vatican telephone exchange.
A Madonna perched on the side wall and a few flowers
in window boxes do their best to give an air of cheerful-
ness. But it remains a forbidding place: heavy iron grilles
protect the ground-floor windows, which anyway are
raised to a safe distance. It looks like a fortress of the
Church defensive. Through the entrance one catches a
glimpse of a dark courtyard where a somewhat melancholy fountain dribbles rather than plays. Schillebeeckx
arrived there just after 8.30 a.m. on Thursday 13 December. He emerged into the December sunshine at about
ten past one. It had been a long morning. He was back
again the next two mornings.

By Saturday 15 December Schillebeeckx and his three
interlocutors were able to sign the minutes of their discussion as a 'true record'. Tape-recorders were not used:
instead two secretaries (male and clerical) kept notes of
what was said. At his own request, Schillebeeckx was
allowed to take away a copy of the minutes. But he was
put at a slight disadvantage in that while he was free
to speak publicly about the colloquy, the other participants were bound by the 'pontifical secret', which is a
particularly secret secret, rather like the seal of the con-

fessional. So Schillebeeckx was in effect put on his honour. He could not attack by name any of the theologians involved in the discussion, since the object of his attack would be unable to reply. And he did not propose to release the text of the minutes until a 'decision', one way or the other, had been reached. Meanwhile, however, we are not completely at a loss. We can reconstruct the gist of what went on by collating an interview Schillebeeckx gave to the Italian weekly *Il Regno* (15 November 1979), the press conference he gave on the afternoon of 15 December, and *Brandpunt-Extra*, a special programme that same evening for KRO, the Dutch Catholic TV station. I should add a note of caution on the *Il Regno* interview. It is invaluable in that it invited Schillebeeckx to comment on each of the nine points in turn; but his answers were brief and no more than preliminary sighting-shots. They should not therefore be taken as expressing Schillebeeckx's complete answer to any of the questions.

Archbishop Jérôme Hamer O.P., Secretary of the CDF, welcomed Schillebeeckx and embraced him warmly. There was a piquant irony about their meeting: for here were two men who were both Dominicans and both Belgians (Schillebeeckx from Antwerp and Hamer from Brussels). They had entered the same province of the Dominicans in the same year, were both professed in September 1935 and ordained – during the German occupation – in August 1941. Their paths had crossed again at Le Saulchoir, the Dominican house of studies near Paris. It would be quite wrong to say (as an American commentator has suggested) that Hamer's jealousy of the success of Schillebeeckx provided the key to the whole affair. But that they were no longer the most congenial of companions would be hard to deny. Those close to Hamer noted his remarkable capacity for 'compartmentalizing' his activities: he could be friendly and charming in a social encounter one day, and write a brutal letter out of duty the next. Each had been shaped by his background. Schillebeeckx had spent twenty-two years in a university setting where questions are asked with a view to discovering what is the case; and he had been deeply

61

involved in the pastoral work of the Dutch Church. Hamer, after a promising early book, *The Church is a Communion* (Eng. trans., 1964), had been called to Rome to work at the Secretariat for Christian Unity. But finding its open-minded approach unsympathetic, he had moved into the more combative world of the CDF. The theologian had become a bureaucrat.

Hamer led Schillebeeckx into the apartments of Cardinal Franjo Seper, Prefect of the CDF, who thanked him for agreeing to come to Rome. Others, it was implied, had been less co-operative. Hans Küng was not mentioned. There were further ironies here. Seper had been Archbishop of Zagreb, Yugoslavia, where he succeeded his friend, Cardinal Stepinac, the victim of Tito's post-war vengeance. He made a series of relatively open-minded speeches at the Second Vatican Council. At the Synod of 1967 he topped the poll in an election to a Commission which was to devise new guidelines for the CDF. This mark of confidence on the part of the world's bishops led Pope Paul VI to summon him to Rome in January 1968 as Prefect of the CDF. As one of the first Slavs to hold a top post in the Vatican, he could be said to have been a precursor of Karol Wojtyla. His appointment was welcomed as evidence that the Curia was being 'internationalized'. But Seper was never very happy in Rome and by December 1979 did not disguise his desire to retire and return to Croatia. He will reach retirement age on 2 October 1980. Meanwhile, he had this unfinished business to conclude.

Hamer then read out the 'protocol' which would govern the discussions. Some of the conditions Schillebeeckx had asked for had been accepted, others not. It had already been agreed that the discussions would be in French. It was also agreed that the original Dutch text of *Jesus – An Experiment in Christology* would be referred to in order to discover exactly what Schillebeeckx had said. Since the colloquy was concerned, officially, with 'clarifications', this was an important point: one could not accept the 'clarifications' or 'distortions' that would inevitably have crept into translations. But perhaps it had been unwise of Schillebeeckx to insist on this condition, since it gravely limited the range of possible interlocutors. One further condition was not accepted. Schillebeeckx had asked that Dr Bas Van Iersel, Dean of the Theology Faculty at Nijmegen, should be present at the discussions. This was not granted, but a compromise was reached: Van Iersel was on hand in a nearby room where he could be consulted if need be. He also came in for the coffee break. Hamer explained the procedure. Each of the three interlocutors – still unidentified – would take three of the topics, make a brief statement and then pose a question on each of them. Schillebeeckx later admitted (*Brandpunt-Extra*) that not knowing until the last moment who his interlocutors would be put great psychological pressure on him. It meant that he was uncertain how to prepare his case in advance. Whereas they had had abundant time to think out and formulate their questions sharply, he could only improvise his answers.

Then, at long last, Schillebeeckx discovered who his three interrogators would be. The first two were Fr Albert Patfoort O.P., Professor at the Dominican Angelicum University in Rome, and Mgr Albert Descamps, Honorary Rector of the University of Louvain and Secretary of the Pontifical Biblical Commission. That did not look too bad. The hearing could be expected to be fair-minded. Patfoort was a noncommittal moderate and Descamps a sound and reliable biblical scholar whose work Schillebeeckx knew. Nor could Descamps be described, except by the hostile, as 'a Roman theologian', and his presence was an indication that the traditional Holy Office practice of having dogmatic theologians sit in judgement over scriptural questions was no longer being slavishly followed. So far so good. But it was the third partner in the colloquy who caused surprise and scandal: it was none other than Fr Jean Galot S.J., whose views we already know.

No legal system in the world – with some exceptions which do not commend the practice – allows a judge to pronounce in advance on a case that he is about to hear. If not a judge who could pass sentence, Galot was at least a *juge d'instruction* who had the task of finding out whether there was a case to answer. But in a broadcast on Vatican Radio on 4 December he had practically called Schillebeeckx a heretic. In answer to a leading question which mentioned the name of Schillebeeckx, he had said that 'some modern theologians deny the divinity of Christ'. The affair was sufficiently serious to make Fr Roberto Tucci S.J., director of Vatican Radio, apologize to Schillebeeckx, and there were reports that Cardinal Agostino Casaroli, Secretary of State, was furious at Galot's ineptitude. Schillebeeckx did the only thing possible: he lodged a protest against the presence of Galot on the grounds that it made an objective discussion impossible. He was told that it came too late. The arrangements had already been made. In any case, his objection did not apply since, once again, he was not 'on trial'. But it was conceded that his protest would be included in the dossier of the case which would be forwarded to the cardinals of the CDF, along with his other objections to the procedure. Galot's clumsy intervention had another consequence to which I will return later.

The colloquy had two other curious features. Everyone involved, apart from the chairman, Mgr Alberto Bovone who is Under-secretary of the CDF (and so Hamer's deputy), was Belgian. The cockpit of Europe had transported itself to the Roman arena. The second oddity was more significant. Schillebeeckx had understood that one of the members of the team would be his so-called 'defence counsel' or spokesman for the author *(relator pro auctore)*. But none of the examiners played that role. Schillebeeckx had been misled: the role of spokesman for the author comes in at an earlier stage – before the author even knows what is happening – and the *ratio agendi* does not say that he should be present at the colloquy. So the 'defence counsel' (to use the improper but convenient legal term once more), though he is supposed to put the author's case, in practice merely serves to permit the proceedings to go ahead in complete secrecy until the time comes to inform the hapless author.

After these alarms, the discussion could begin. The

tone of the meeting was not uncivilized. 'It was', said Schillebeeckx at his press conference, 'friendly, perhaps too friendly. It wasn't at all like a tribunal – but it wasn't a farce either. The discussions were very rigorous even though there wasn't time to go into much depth.'

Fr Patfoort began with the theme of revelation and faith. In his interview in *Il Regno*, Schillebeeckx had commented on revelation as follows:

> In my two christological books [*Jesus – An Experiment in Christology* and *Gnade und Befreiung* ('Grace and Freedom') so far only available in German] I emphasized human experience. Where there is a revelation, it affects the people who are involved in a human experience. So one cannot oppose revelation on the one hand to human experience on the other. Revelation does not make sense without human experience and it is expressed in human terms and by means of human concepts and images.

Schillebeeckx was here opposing the concept of revelation as a special kind of 'inside information' about God. His simple point is the one found in the Thomistic adage: 'Whatever is received is received according to the capacity of the receiver.' Revelation does not permit us to jump out of our skins or out of our own age. Patfoort could well have insisted: 'But does revelation speak of God or of man?' And Schillebeeckx would certainly have replied that this was a false dilemma: to speak of man and his destiny is already to speak of God: anthropology opens out into theology.

Patfoort moved on to the normative value of Church councils and the Pope's infallible teaching authority. On this Schillebeeckx had said:

> I did not discuss these questions in my books.... It is this silence that is found unacceptable. I confined myself to the exegesis of the New Testament, and did not consider the Christian tradition as a whole. I make a synthesis on the basis of the New Testament, and this gives rise to the idea that I neglect the importance of the papal *magisterium*.

One cannot deal with everything at once. One can have

limited aims and restricted goals, and a theologian does not have to apologize for confining himself, even methodologically, to the New Testament. But Schillebeeckx would certainly have been pressed to fill out this answer, and no doubt did so along the lines suggested on p. 55 above: a conciliar pronouncement such as that of Nicaea may be legitimate and normative and yet require completing by another strand of reflection that was present in the New Testament sources and yet had been unduly neglected.

Patfoort's final question concerned the pre-existence of the Word and Jesus as the Son of God. On this Schillebeeckx had said in *Il Regno*:

This is a rather abstract question. I do not speak of the pre-existence of Christ in my book, but I accept the great theological symbolism contained in the affirmation that Christ as Jesus is called Son of God. But does this mean that we have to say that he was the Son of God before being Jesus? These are very abstract speculations. In fact I don't speak about them in my book. These are questions about my silences.

The question – and Schillebeeckx's answer to it – reveal the great gulf in theological method. For when Schillebeeckx says that x or y are 'abstract' questions, he does not mean that they are unimportant or trivial. He means rather that they do not fall within his scope which is to present a *functional* Jesus (i.e. the interest focuses on 'what he does for us and for our salvation') rather than an intemporal ontological description of him.

Then came the coffee break. It cannot have been easy to move from an interrogation which could have the gravest consequences to relaxed social conversation. Schillebeeckx reports that during one break Mgr Bovone said to him: 'I am so glad that you came to Rome, because it is a good thing when we can see a theologian face to face and learn how committed he is to the faith of the Church.' That was reassuring, – or was it? Schillebeeckx later wondered whether the excessive politeness and friendliness were not the most menacing aspect of the whole meeting.

In any case, after the coffee break, Fr Galot took over the questioning, and it would not be surprising if the atmosphere became a little more strained. The heart of the matter was being approached. What did Schillebeeckx think of 'the sacrificial value of the death of Jesus'? To *Il Regno* he had said:

> This is the age-old question of 'satisfaction'. It is often said that the sin of man was so great that it required the death of the Son of God to put it right. That is no longer acceptable. But I do not, however, deny the sacrificial and 'satisfactory' value of the death of Jesus Christ.... To deny that would be to deny God's gratuitous love. But it was not God who sentenced his Son to death: Jesus Christ was killed by human beings.

Galot's task was not to refute but to ascertain. So he may have been able to say *'transeat'* to that answer and move on to the next and, for him, most crucial question: was Jesus aware of being the Messiah and the Son of God? In his interview, Schillebeeckx had said:

> This is a purely historical question. If perhaps Christ did not know that he was the Son of God, that does not prevent us from asserting and believing it. But it is a historical question which has nothing to do with faith. There are historians – and I was trying to write historically – who say that Jesus was not conscious of being the Messiah in the regal sense of Jewish expectations. But they hold that he had an awareness of being messianic, prophetic and eschatological.

Schillebeeckx, in fact, takes a different starting-point in his discussion of the 'consciousness' or 'self-awareness' of Jesus, and he is much less sceptical than many historians. He maintains that the key to understanding Jesus is his '*Abba*-experience', the abiding sense of closeness to and unity with the Father expressed in his historically original and unique mode of address, *Abba, Father*. This unbreakable intimacy with the Father is such that it cannot be broken even by death. It is in this sense that Schillebeeckx speaks of Jesus as 'Son of God': 'In his humanity Jesus is so intimately "of the Father" that by virtue of this very intimacy he is "Son of God"' (*Jesus – An Experiment in Christology*, p. 658). Or again, without the inverted commas: 'Jesus of Nazareth, the crucified-and-risen One, is the Son of God in the fashion of an actual and contingent human being' (ibid., p. 668).

The Thursday morning session concluded with the question: did Jesus found the Church? Schillebeeckx's comment on this point in *Il Regno* was:

> I do not deny this in my book. I simply said that Christ thought the world was about to come to an end. So he didn't have a plan to found a Church, he simply brought together the twelve apostles. But that in itself *was* the foundation of the Church, especially when confirmed by the resurrection.

This rather abrupt statement can be filled out by Schillebeeckx's discussion of the vocation of the Twelve in *Jesus — An Experiment in Christology*:

> In the pre-Easter situation the 'call' of Jesus was already unique: in Jesus' 'call' to 'go after him' we have perhaps the clearest evidence of his role as an eschatological prophet of the imminent rule of God. It shatters every frame of the 'master-disciple' relationship, because it is a conclusive, latter-day act on the part of the eschatological prophet; it serves to condense his call to *metanoia* (change of heart) into an eschatological *metanoia* as a disciple of Jesus, a vocation to total commitment, burning all one's boats in the service of the kingdom to come. (p. 219)

In the post-Easter period Jesus is perceived not only as the one who can call, absolutely, but also as 'the one filled with God's Spirit' (ibid., p. 441). Response to his call, in the Spirit, constitutes henceforward the gathering of God's new people which we call the Church. This is an approach to the ecclesiological question which avoids the pitfalls of anachronism.

The second session took place on Friday morning, 14 December. Mgr Descamps took Schillebeeckx through the three remaining questions. On the institution of the Eucharist, he had said to the *Il Regno* interviewer:

> I discussed this at length in my book, because there are several strata or levels in the accounts that we find in

the Synoptics and St Paul. H. Schürmann and many other exegetes say this. I agree with them that these are liturgical words. That is unanimously accepted. So they are not words said by Christ in person. Rome does not accept that ...

So Schillebeeckx knew that this point, would cause trouble. The same was true of the next question on the 'virginal conception of Jesus'. He had said to *Il Regno*:

In my book I say that this doctrine is found in Matthew alone and that the other evangelists do not speak about it. And I explain what the expression means. But in the book I don't say what I think about it. I simply say that it is a very peripheral question for christology. I note that there was a tendency in the primitive Christian tradition – though it was not universal – to hold that the Son of God became man without a virginal conception. And I discuss what it means to call a child the Son of God. Nothing more.

This answer could easily be misconstrued – and it was in several newspapers. To say that the virginal conception of Jesus is 'a very peripheral question for christology' is not a denial of it: it is to say that christological faith does not depend upon it, which is evident since Paul, whose 'high' christology is not in doubt, does not allude to the virginal conception.

If the 'virginal conception' had not been dealt with at any length in *Jesus – An Experiment in Christology*, the same cannot be said of 'the objective reality of the resurrection', the final topic raised by Mgr Descamps. For the whole of Part 3 ('Christian interpretation of the crucified-and-risen One') is devoted to a study of the resurrection. Schillebeeckx's answer to *Il Regno* briefly summarized his position:

This is the big question. The objective reality of the resurrection is evident. And it is evident in my book. But I don't place the stress on the empty tomb or on the appearances. I merely say that the genesis of faith in the resurrection is a sort of *metanoia*, a conversion experience, after the death of the Lord. It involves the conversion of the apostles who, after his death, experienced his spiritual or pneumatic power and presence. And they wrote that down in the form of appearance stories. But for me the appearances as such are not the foundation of faith. But I do not deny the objectivity of the experience.

That, of course, would only be the opening statement in what could have been a lengthy debate. *Jesus – An Experiment in Christology* (pp. 518–44 especially) shows the various ways in which Schillebeeckx could have elaborated and defended his position. Its most notable characteristic is that he is concerned with understanding what 'resurrection' meant and could mean in the light of Jewish thinking, and not with apologetics. At the same time he is fully aware of how far 'what happened in Jesus' is original and breaks through the available Jewish categories, imposing new meanings on them. The conclusion to this section is the clearest statement of New Testament christological faith: 'Jesus of Nazareth is the Christ, that is the one totally filled with God's eschatological Spirit. He is the latter-day and definitive revelation of God and in being so is at the same time the paradigm of an "eschatological humanity"' (ibid., p. 544).

The interrogation was at an end. It remained only to draw up and approve the summary of the discussions. The main work on this was completed by the evening of Friday 14 December. Next morning Schillebeeckx was up early and writing furiously, for the protocol allowed for after-thoughts and precisions to be included in the minutes. Then he went along to the CDF for the last time. It took about two and a half hours to work through the minutes. Schillebeeckx was somewhat alarmed to find that new questions had been introduced at this eleventh hour; and there was one awkward moment. It came when one of his interlocutors (evidently Galot, but Schillebeeckx would not name him) said: 'I note that you say you believe in the divinity of Jesus, but that is not what I find in your book.' Schillebeeckx kept his cool and replied: 'If that is your personal judgement, you have the right to hold it, but I do not agree.' Schillebeeckx's final condition had been accepted. He asked to be allowed to take away a copy of the minutes so that they could not be tampered with later without his knowledge.

But had he, in the time-honoured phrase, 'satisfied the examiners'? Candidates are notoriously bad judges of their own performance, and in this particular examination what might have seemed to Schillebeeckx a telling point could have been differently judged by his interlocutors. They were not testing his knowledge of scriptures or the Christian tradition but simply his orthodoxy. But he emerged convinced that on most of the important questions he had been able to reach agreement. He made frequent use, as he does in his book, of the distinction between matters of history and matters of faith, and he insisted that there were no differences on matters of faith. What remaining differences there were belonged to the order of *interpretation*. 'We all accept', said Schillebeeckx at his press conference on the afternoon of 15 December, 'that Jesus is "true God and true man". But the problem is how we are to express this truth today. The word "person", for example, has changed its meaning and therefore we have to find a different way of putting Chalcedon so that it will make sense for our contemporaries.' But he seemed a little less confident in his KRO interview – it had been a long day. Asked whether he thought he had provided the asked-for clarifications, he said: 'I clarified the questions in much the same way that I did in my written answer. Whether that now brings more light than my written text remains uncertain.'

But there was another factor, external to the colloquy, which had greatly encouraged Schillebeeckx. On Tuesday evening, 11 December, Cardinal Jo Willebrands had spoken on KRO's *Brandpunt* programme, and declared his support for Schillebeeckx. He did not mince his words:

I ám convinced that Schillebeeckx does not teach heretical doctrines or doctrines that deviate from orthodoxy. Those who make such accusations have no right to attack a theologian of such quality ... Schillebeeckx is one of the few theologians in the Church today who have a profound knowledge of the whole tradition of

71

theology: he has a deep understanding of scripture which is the foundation of theology, of the patristic and scholastic periods, and of modern developments ...

I have a high regard for Schillebeeckx. His teaching is the fruit of his Christian faith and his dedication to the Church. There are few theologians in the Church who are on his level. He is dear to me because of his faith and his service to the Church.

I hope that the Schillebeeckx case will be resolved favourably. But if it comes before the cardinals of the CDF, I promise to be present at the meeting and to defend him.

This support from the man who wore several hats – he is President of the Dutch Episcopal Conference, Chancellor of the Catholic University of Nijmegen, President of the Secretariat for Christian Unity, and one of the ten cardinal members of the CDF – was most welcome. It was also completely unexpected.

For in mid-November, only a month before, Willebrands had told Schillebeeckx that he would go on TV if necessary but only to 'explain the procedure' and that it was his duty to remain silent and neutral on the theological questions proper. Something had evidently persuaded him to change his mind. Various explanations were offered. Willebrands, it was suggested, truthfully, is a prudent man who does not take undue risks: therefore he could not have made his statement without previous approval from Pope John Paul – and they had abundant time to discuss the matter in plane and helicopter during the papal visit to Turkey. Moreover, John Paul is known to have a high regard for Willebrands, whom he needs if his project of union with the Orthodox is ever to be realized. This was a highly plausible theory. But it was open to one grave objection: it does not fit in with what we know of John Paul's views on theology and theologians (cf. Chapter 6).

Schillebeeckx offered a different explanation. He suspected that Willebrands' change of mind 'might not be unconnected' with Galot's inept attack on Vatican Radio. The fact that someone so closely involved in the procedure as Galot should have taken a public stand in advance of the colloquy seems to have liberated Willebrands from his scruples and galvanized him into action. Unfairness makes him angry. The rules – the decencies even – were not being obeyed. So he, too, decided to make his position known and to play it rough. But the consequences of his action are incalculable. When a 'decision' is reached in the Schillebeeckx case, it will be Willebrands as his Ordinary who has the task of communicating it to him. In the case of a negative verdict, will Willebrands, in conscience, be able to pass it on? He can of course act merely as a letter-box. But could he carry out the decision if, say, it meant dismissing Schillebeeckx from the Catholic University of Nijmegen? Or would resignation be the only honourable course? These are speculative questions, but they make it clear beyond any doubt that the Schillebeeckx case has implications for the future not only of Schillebeeckx but for the Church in Holland and the whole ecumenical movement.

But all speculation aside, the intervention of Willebrands means that when the Schillebeeckx case comes before the ten cardinals of the CDF, they will not be unanimous. That is the next stage of the procedure. The ten cardinals will receive the whole dossier, including the previous written material, the minutes of the colloquy and the various protests of Schillebeeckx. A glance at their names does not make one sanguine as to the outcome. They are Franjo Seper, Agostino Casaroli, Wladislaw Rubin, Sebastiano Baggio, Angelo Rossi, Gabriel-Marie Garrone, William Wakefield Baum, Pericle Felici, Josef Schröffer and Jo Willebrands. It is not unfair to say that none of them has made any notable contribution to theological studies, though a number of them (including Schröffer and Garrone) were theology professors in the 1940s. Baggio is outstanding in that it is said that he has not opened a serious work of theology in the last twenty years. Felici is noted for his work on the revision of the code of canon law – but that is not the best preparation for New Testament studies. With the exception of Willebrands, all reside in Rome. They would certainly be capable of a sensible judgement on a quasi-political question (e.g. should Lefebvre be rehabilitated and under what conditions?), but one is less convinced of their ability to handle a strenuous theological problem.

Yet these are the men who have to 'decide the matter' (the *ratio agendi* is as vague as that) and make their recommendation for action to the Pope. If there is a split vote, the Pope will be informed of that as well. We already know, from the Willebrands statement, that there will be a division, at least 1–9. In rough order of severity, the possible courses of action are: a private warning to be more circumspect in future; a public warning (known as a *monitum*) along the same lines; a withdrawal of the 'canonical mission' (the fate of Hans Küng) which would mean that Schillebeeckx could no longer be considered as a 'Catholic theologian' and would have to cease teaching at Nijmegen. Still stronger penalties such as forcible laicization or – at the limit – excommunication, seem unlikely. Or there might be stalling tactics, not foreseen by the procedure: requests for still further 'clarifications' and possibly a meeting with the group of cardinals itself (unlikely: there is a limit to the process of endless 'clarifications'). No one can predict in advance what the decision will be, since there are no rules governing it. Nor is there any form of appeal against the eventual decision.

At the press conference of 15 December, Schillebeeckx was asked whether he would revise his book if it were condemned. He replied: 'When I have said that something is white, I cannot say that it is not white. It is true that there is obedience ... But I do not fear the sort of condemnation that Jacques Pohier had.' He meant that he did not *expect* a Pohier-like condemnation (with a ban on public lectures and presiding at the Eucharist in public). In any case, nothing will happen very swiftly. Hamer told Schillebeeckx at their final meeting that the decision would take some time. He quoted the old Latin pun, *Roma mora* (Rome means delay). Public opinion will be allowed time to move on to other, less recondite matters.

So the Dominican Hamer said goodbye to his brother

Dominican Schillebeeckx. It was difficult not to recall the words of yet another Dominican, Père Clérissac, who wrote to the French novelist Georges Bernanos at the height of the Modernist crisis, when a spying system and a veritable reign of terror operated against theological innovators. *'Ce n'est rien de souffrir pour l'Eglise,'* said Clérissac, *'il faut avoir souffert par elle'* ('It is easy to suffer for the Church, the difficult thing is to suffer at the hands of the Church'). There are many precedents of theologians emerging, later in life, from a cloud of suspicion. John Henry Newman became a cardinal. Yves Congar O.P. and Henri de Lubac S.J. were both forbidden to teach in the early 1950s only to become *periti* of great influence at the Second Vatican Council. At Schillebeeckx's press conference, a somewhat flustered journalist addressed him by mistake as 'Cardinal Schillebeeckx'. 'That is a little premature', said Schillebeeckx. It was the only moment of light relief in an otherwise grim affair.

That Saturday I had lunch with René Laurentin, one of the best-known theologians and reporters of France. 'Schillebeeckx', he suggested gloomily, 'is better at doing theology than at answering questions. His replies are not subtle enough. He walks naïvely into traps.' And he contrasted this evangelical simplicity – the simplicity of the dove without the cunning of the serpent – with Hans Küng's verbal agility. 'Küng', he said, 'is a Houdini who can extricate himself from the tightest corner.' The comparison seemed true enough at the time and I agreed with it. But already it was out of date, and falsified by a secret event that had taken place that same day.

5. *And then there was Kung*

What is requested from defenders of the traditional
teaching is not a condemnation of the book *(Infallible?)* but a refutation. If this can be provided, then
a condemnation is unnecessary; if it cannot be
provided, then a condemnation is unjustified.
> Patrick McGrath in *The Tablet*, 3 July 1971

The Press Office of the Vatican is normally a rather
somnent place. But on the morning of 18 December 1979
there was an 'event'. Cardinal Bernadin Gantin and Fr
Roger Heckel S.J., President and Secretary of the Pontifical Justice and Peace Commission, were busily 'presenting' Pope John Paul II's Message for World Peace Day
which was arranged for 1 January 1980. That is to say
that they summarized it at unnecessary length and answered some rather desultory questions about it. The
questions were desultory because, although no one is
openly opposed to peace, it is not a topic to set the blood
racing. It seemed more important to study it than to
ask superfluous questions about it. It was a vigorous
document which denounced the technique of the 'big
lie' in international politics:

> One of the big lies that poison relations between indivi-
> duals and groups consists in ignoring all aspects of an
> opponent's action, even the good and just ones, for
> the sake of condemning him more completely. (No. 6)

That seemed to fit the Schillebeeckx case with some
precision, right down to the distinction made by the CDF
between 'subjective intentions' and 'objective impact'.
There was more:

> What should one say on the practice of combating or
> silencing those who do not share the same views by
> labelling them as enemies, attributing to them hostile

intentions, and using skilful and instant propaganda to brand them as aggressors? (No. 1)

What should one say? One should say firmly that they are wrong, and ought henceforward to desist from such deplorable practices.

At this point a friend slipped in and whispered in my ear: 'You're wasting your time here. Hurry. Hans Küng has been shot down in flames.' The irony was almost too painful to bear. The news quickly spread round the hall. Gantin and Heckel continued to answer questions ('Was the criticism of East and West even-handed?') but their audience silently melted away. The condemnation of Küng was a more important story than any pontifical exhortation to truth-telling and peace. It was futile of Vatican officials to complain that the media concentrate on artificially worked-up scandals at the expense of solid and important pronouncements on major issues of the day. There was no doubt what the headlines would be the next day, and for months to come.

The document which 'shot down Küng in flames' was a declaration of the Congregation for the Doctrine of Faith (text in Appendix 2). It had been signed by Cardinal Seper on Saturday 15 December, three days before. So while Schillebeeckx was checking over the minutes of his conversation with the three experts of the CDF in one room, in another room of this self-same palace Seper was putting his name to a document designed to end the career of Hans Küng as a Catholic theologian. The declaration said that 'Küng has departed from the integral truth of Catholic faith, and therefore can no longer be considered as a Catholic theologian nor function as such in a teaching role'. The CDF declaration was backed up by another signed by Cardinal Joseph Höffner on behalf of the German Bishops (text in Appendix 3), which gave a more detailed version of past events and concluded with the important precision that Küng 'remained a priest and a Catholic'. He was thus relegated to a rather curious limbo where he could *be* a priest and a Catholic but not actually *utter* as one.

But oddity apart, it was a severe punishment. Whereas Schillebeeckx could be considered on the verge of retirement, the Swiss-born Küng was only fifty-one years old. If the declaration were to be acted upon it would have the effect of cutting off his theological activity in his prime. No one explained why the declaration was dated 15 December but not released until 18 December. Perhaps the German Bishops needed more time to complete their statement. Perhaps some PR genius thought that public attention would be more concerned with the coming of Christmas and the season of good will than with the mishaps of Catholic theologians. But the condemnation of Küng was widely taken to mean that Schillebeeckx should not be thought of as an individual case. To denounce one theologian may be a misfortune; to take on two in a week looks like an act of deliberate policy.

That was not how the CDF saw the matter. Archbishop Jérôme Hamer wearily complained about overwork. He behaved rather in the manner of a harassed GP in a 'flu epidemic ('There's an awful lot of error about the place this winter'). The Vatican Press Office put out a statement of quite extraordinary blandness. The question would naturally arise, it conceded, as to whether the CDF measures taken against three theologians (Pohier was the third) were part of some overall scheme. To which the official answer was: 'This is not so, and one must regard the fact as a pure coincidence.' One wondered if one had heard correctly: 'A pure coincidence?' 'Yes,' came the answer, 'a pure coincidence.' The statement further explained: 'One should emphasize that all three cases are different. Each one has to be treated separately, and it would be artificial to explain them as though they were associated with each other.' Of course they were different. But the common factor was that they all involved theologians and the CDF, and that nothing like this had been seen since the end of the Council in 1965.

The improbable disclaimers did not help the already fast-dwindling stock of credibility possessed by the CDF. Yet one had to concede that the Küng case differed in certain important respects from that of Schillebeeckx.

The main difference was that while the Küng declaration represented the *conclusion* of a one-sided process, the Schillebeeckx hearing was merely a *stage* in a process that had been to some extent publicly discussed. But that merely meant that while slight hope remained for Schillebeeckx, there was none at all for Küng. Küng had been sentenced – and there was no appeal; Schillebeeckx was awaiting his sentence.

A second distinction lay in their attitude to the official procedures. Although protesting all the while, Schillebeeckx had followed the rules faithfully, almost scrupulously. Küng had both protested against the procedure and refused to go along with it. He had therefore put himself in the wrong. He had refused, as the Vatican Press Office statement said, 'repeated invitations to take part in a conversation'. However, it was not strictly accurate to say that Küng had refused to engage in dialogue. He had made his position clear from 1973 onwards. He was prepared at any time for a true dialogue. But he was not prepared to accept a conversation under the conditions that were imposed. This was not because he was disobedient or curmudgeonly. It was because he believed that Church procedures should not be more unjust than civil procedures. He therefore requested that he should see his dossier in advance and know who his accusers were; that he should know who had been appointed to defend him; and that there should be a right of appeal against any eventual judgement. These conditions were not met, so he stayed away. There was a not particularly subtle distinction between saying 'Küng refused to dialogue' and 'Küng did not consider that he was being offered a true dialogue'. But it was widely ignored.

Another major difference between Schillebeeckx and Küng concerned the errors they were thought to have perpetrated. While the Schillebeeckx hearing concentrated on one book and one theme – christology – the two declarations on Küng raised a wide variety of topics, some taken from the past and others from the immediate present. The result was that it was a little difficult to focus on the central complaint. The declaration raked over past history when it recalled the February 1975 document of the CDF which had said that 'Küng was opposed, in different degrees, to the doctrine of the Church which must be held by all the faithful'. That statement had singled out his views on infallibility in the Church, the *magisterium*'s unique role in the interpretation of the deposit of faith, and the conditions for the valid celebration of the Eucharist. Even in 1975 this was a barrel-scraping list, since the last 'error' (said to be contrary not only to Vatican II but to the Fourth Lateran Council) was originally propounded in a book published in 1967 (*The Church*, Burns and Oates). An error cannot be deemed to be very dangerous if it takes eight years to get round to condemning it. In any case, the alleged 'error' did not exist: Küng had merely said that the question of a non-ordained person celebrating the Eucharist in an emergency was 'at least debatable', which seems a blameless enough suggestion.

The main emphasis, in the declaration, is on infallibility. Küng is said to reduce it to 'a certain indefectibility of the Church in truth, with the possibility of error in doctrinal statements which the *magisterium* of the Church teaches must be held definitively'. But the declaration does not confine itself to infallibility. It adds that Küng does 'serious harm to some essential points of Catholic faith (e.g. those teachings which pertain to the consubstantiality of Christ with his Father, and to the Blessed Virgin Mary)'. These are much graver charges and would bring Küng much closer to Schillebeeckx. But they are merely alluded to *en passant*, there is no serious discussion of them, and no evidence is provided. This is a somewhat cavalier procedure in a document which has such serious consequences. It is as though someone had decided to 'get Küng' and was not too scrupulous about how it was to be done. Alternatively one can adopt the CDF view that error so abounds in the works of Küng that a detailed spelling out is unnecessary: but then we are worse off than before. The incriminated theologian does not know which charges to answer and moves in a Kafkaesque world of darkness and mystery.

80

The declaration also had to answer the question: why precisely *now*? For on its own admission, these 'errors' had been around for some time. In what way had Küng added to the stock of error? The answer of the declaration was that Küng had not devised any new errors (or at least none had been detected or were worth mentioning), but that he had persisted in repeating the old errors in even sharper and more explicit form. The two most recent works cited as evidence of this 'intensification of error' were *Kirche – Gehalten in der Wahrheit?* ('The Church, Maintained in the Truth?', Benziger, 1979) and his introduction to August B. Hasler's *Wie der Papst unfehlbar wurde* ('How the Pope became Infallible', Piper, 1979). These were the straws that broke the camel's back. They provided evidence that Küng had not shown the slightest sign of the repentance which he had promised way back in 1975. The CDF's stance was that it had displayed remarkable patience and almost superhuman forbearance. Since 1975 it had 'refrained from further action regarding the above-mentioned opinions of Professor Küng, presuming that he himself would abandon them. But since this presumption no longer exists ...' his faculty to teach as a Catholic theologian was withdrawn. So the present condemnation was based on a 'sharpening' of earlier opinions found in the two works referred to. Since *Kirche – Gehalten in der Wahrheit?* takes the form of a meditation on the mystery of the Church's enduring dwelling in truth, and is a work of spirituality rather than theology proper, the emphasis must fall on the introduction to Hasler's provocative book.

Here Küng's critique of the doctrine of infallibility is said by the German bishops to be 'sharper'. Judging degrees of 'sharpness' or 'asperity' is a delicate enterprise. It does not seem that the February 1979 introduction to Hasler's book marks any notable advance, from the point of view of 'sharpness', on *Infallible?* which was published in 1971. Küng's style had always been waspish. It had been criticized for that reason by Karl Rahner S.J. as long ago as 1970 (when he spoke of Küng's 'hard, aggressive mode of expression': *Stimmen der Zeit*, 'Kritik an Hans Küng', December 1970, p. 362). Nearly ten years had gone by and Küng welcomed the invitation to write a preface to Hasler's book as an opportunity to draw up a 'balance sheet' of the infallibility debate in the intervening period (or more precisely since his last 'balance sheet' published in 1973). He addressed himself to the question: has the debate on infallibility been bogged down or has it moved on?

Küng thought that it had progressed on four major points. First the legitimacy of asking questions about infallibility was now more widely recognized. It was no longer regarded as disreputable. His book *Infallible?* had been understood as an act of 'Her Majesty's loyal opposition' coming from within the household of faith. Too many theologians had wearied of providing 'opportunistic interpretations' of Vatican I's teaching. They had tied themselves in knots explaining what infallibility did not mean – so much·so that the doctrine of Vatican I had in fact died the death of a thousand qualifications. Theologians had therefore concluded that it was much better to bring the question out into the open. The habit of claiming that a text said the opposite of what in fact it plainly asserted was characteristic, Küng noted, not with the greatest of tact, 'of all totalitarian systems, and it obscures the problem, offends against intellectual honesty, and delays an eventual solution' (ibid., p. XVI). It is difficult to gainsay Küng on this point, polemics aside: infallibility is on the agenda of many Catholic theologians.

His second claim is less convihcing. It is that Catholic theologians have been more ready to accept that the *magisterium* has in fact made mistakes, and that this admission undermines the doctrine of infallibility. What is true is that Catholic theologians have become more conscious – thanks in great measure to Küng – that language is partial, threatened, inadequate, time-conditioned, liable to misunderstanding and so on, but that there is a crucial difference between a *poorly formulated* dogmatic statement and an *erroneous* one. Küng is on surer ground when he says that Catholic theologians have become sceptical about the usefulness and value of the concept of 'infallible' itself. This is true. So much so that no new infallible pronouncements are expected, and the Irishism that 'infallibility would not now be defined unless it already had been defined' is now common currency. Pope John XXIII did not forfeit any authority because he refused to make any 'infallible' statements. But the suspicion of 'infallible' does not lead Catholic theologians – or Küng – to abandon the contention that the Church remains and dwells in the truth.

According to Küng, the debate on infallibility has also helped to clarify what is the central point at issue. Here is how Küng defines it:

Are there certain statements (dogmas, definitions, judgements, propositions of faith) which are not only in fact true (which is not in dispute) but are *infallibly* true, and infallibly true because certain office-holders in certain circumstances have the special assistance of the Holy Spirit so that in advance they cannot go wrong? (pp. XVIII–XIX)

The central question, in other words, is the validity of the definition of Vatican I which says that there are such statements guaranteed in the way described. The 'target', in short, is the Vatican I definition.

Küng's fourth and final reflection is that recent research has, wholly unexpectedly, confirmed his own positions on infallibility. This holds true in three main areas: scripture studies, patristics, and medieval history. A word on each.

First, Catholic theologians and exegetes no longer attempt to base 'infallibility' on the well-known passages of scripture which speak of Peter as rock, as confirming the faith of his brethren or as feeding the lambs and sheep. That is an anachronistic venture that has long since been abandoned. What they have done, in exchange, is to try to work out the meaning of the 'Petrine Ministry' in the New Testament and for our time. The 'Petrine Ministry' is shown to have more flexibility and pliability than was supposed, and the way is open for its renewal today. But that says nothing about infallibility.

Secondly, work on the ancient councils of the Church has shown that the Fathers did not operate with any concept of infallibility. True, an ecumenical council such as Nicaea (325) was held to say what was true, but for very different reasons. Küng summarizes:

> A council spoke the truth, not because there were no juridical objections to its summoning, nor because it assembled the majority of the world's bishops, nor because it was confirmed by any human authority of any kind, nor because it had the extraordinary assistance of the Holy Spirit, nor because *a priori* it could not be mistaken. On the contrary it spoke the truth because in spite of new terms it did not utter anything new, because it handed on the old tradition in a new language, because it bore witness to the original message, because it breathed the atmosphere of scripture, because it was backed up by the Gospel. (p. XX)

This, it should be noted, does not make the authority of the council any less authentic or binding, on the contrary. But it does not make its authority depend upon the supposed property of 'infallibility'.

Thirdly, medieval historians (especially the American Brian Tierney) have shown that 'infallibility' came into currency not as the result of a long and steady development but as a sudden creation towards the end of the thirteenth century. Infallibility was the invention of an eccentric Franciscan, Petrus Olivi, who died in 1298. He was frequently accused of heresy, and in 1324 Pope John XXII said that his work was of the devil, the father of lies. Even counter-Reformation popes could not appeal to an unquestioned tradition of infallibility, which is why Trent did not even consider defining the doctrine. 'Infallibility', Küng concludes with C. Langlois, 'is essentially a nineteenth-century idea.'

In the light of all these considerations Küng concludes his preface to Hasler's book with the suggestion, originally put forward by Yves Congar O.P., that 'under the new pontificate, the question of infallibility should be examined afresh, exegetically, historically and theologically, with scientific honesty, a sense of fair play and justice' (p. XXXIV). To this end he proposed that an ecumenical commission should be set up. Its members should be experts knowledgeable in the various relevant areas. He added that the emphasis should fall not on the negative aspects of the question but rather on the positive side. In this way the fact that the Church 'remains in the truth despite error' would be better grounded in the Christian message and the Catholic tradition, 'and so better lived in the life of the Church today'. Unless one has a mind made up in advance, that does not sound like the statement of someone who wishes to disrupt the Church. On the contrary, it suggests someone who wishes to serve the Church. The question of infallibility has been posed. It is on the agenda. It cannot be repressed or swept under the carpet. It ought therefore to be tackled with the best intellectual resources available.

Yet it was this text – the introduction to Hasler's book – which provoked the CDF to take action. After this it could bear no more. Its patience and forbearance were at an end. So despite the mention of various other errors, it was Küng's views on infallibility, repeated 'more explicitly', that are the principal cause of his condemnation. Let us accept that this was the real reason. Four reflections then suggest themselves.

Küng's views on 'infallibility' are the main grounds for complaint. But 'infallibility', whatever one may think about it, does not have a high priority in the hierarchy of Catholic theological questions. The Second Vatican Council declared that 'in Catholic teaching there exists an order or hierarchy of truths, since they vary in their relationship to the foundation of Christian faith' (On Ecumenism, No. 11). Infallibility is not only not at the top of that hierarchy of truths, but it cannot be, for if it were, it would have been very remiss of the Church to wait until 1870 to define something deemed to be so close to 'the foundation of Christian faith'. This does not mean that 'infallibility' is a trivial or unimportant question. It has a modest place. As Avery Dulles S.J., one of the most moderate of theologians, remarked: 'The life of the Catholic Christian is by no means centred on the papacy; it ought, at least, to be centred on God and Jesus Christ' (*The Resilient Church*, 1978, p. 113).

Secondly, it is not difficult to understand why the work of Hasler, *How the Pope became Infallible*, was not welcome to the Vatican. It was a popular abridgement of the author's larger two-volume work (*Pius IX, päpstliche Unfehlbarkeit und I Vatikanisches Konzil*, Anton Hiersemann, Stuttgart, 1977), and it set out to answer historically the important question: how was it that a doctrine not universally held in the Church could be defined by Vatican I? Hasler's answer is that the Fathers of Vatican I were not really free, and that they were manipulated by Pope Pius IX, whose profound conviction of his own infallibility was greatly strengthened by visions of a particularly dubious and unhealthy kind. Hasler, moreover, raises frankly the question of whether Pius IX was entirely sane: he had suffered from epilepsy in youth, his piety verged on superstition, his grasp on theology was negligible ('I am tradition', he is reported to have said), he was given to outbursts of anger against anyone who disagreed with him, and he was inaccessible to rational argument on any issue. Hasler's conclusion is that the minority at Vatican I had the better historical arguments, as subsequent scholarship has confirmed, but that they were never allowed to present their case properly. The book is certainly polemical in intent and style, and it drags in some unverifiable hypotheses – notably that the Dominican Cardinal Filippo Maria Guidi, one of the opponents of the infallibility decree at Vatican I, was the natural son of Pius IX, thus bringing to the theological confrontation the added dimension of the Oedipus conflict (p. 61).

But the main theme of the book is serious and scholarly. The CDF could not be expected to appreciate Hasler's work (which began when he was a member of the Secretariat for Christian Unity, to which he had been called by Cardinal Augustin Bea in 1966). Küng's enthusiastic endorsement of Hasler would not have helped his own case. Hasler, meantime, a priest from the diocese of Sankt Gallen in Switzerland, is also being dealt with, but by administrative measures. It is believed that his Bishop has been asked to reduce him to the lay state, forcibly and against his will. These are sad personal details. They are relevant, however, to the wider question in this way: if Hasler's historical work and Küng's exploitation of it are to be challenged and refuted, they have to be challenged and refuted on *historical* grounds. *A priori* answers cannot be given to the problems they raise. Still less can they be resolved by disciplinary methods.

A third reflection on the choice of 'infallibility' as the grounds for condemning Küng is that, despite his claim that a consensus was building up in favour of his positions, many Catholic theologians have had and have expressed their reservations. This is perfectly normal. Küng advances arguments and has them challenged by his peers. The notion that Catholic theologians hasten to fall flat on their faces in unbounded admiration for the master from Tübingen is a preposterous fantasy. The principle so frequently stated in Chapter 1, that theologians are best judged by their peers, fits the Küng case with some precision. But they can *no longer perform this necessary task*, once Küng has been condemned. The question is removed from the realm of academic discussion and turned into a loyalty test.

Theologians have not, on the whole, disputed Küng's right to ask questions about infallibility, since they are in the business of asking questions themselves. But they have also asked questions about the validity of his arguments and the limitations of his proposed solutions. I will mention two. Küng's original case on the impossibility of their being 'infallible propositions' at all depends ultimately on a view of truth derived from Hegel which involves saying that 'a proposition can be both true and false' (*Infallible?*, p. 140). The Protestant theologian George A. Lindbeck of Yale, said that this position is logically and philosophically dangerous for Christian faith, for it involves accepting 'a highly speculative and technical philosophical view of truth as the basis of his case against a wrong interpretation of infallibility' ('A Protestant Perspective', *America*, 24 April 1971, p. 83). Küng has never really managed to answer this difficulty. It is a major obstacle to understanding him. In any case for *most of the time* he makes use of a more conventional two-valued logic (identity, contradiction, excluded middle and so on) so that when he calls *Humanae Vitae* erroneous it cannot simultaneously be true. But when he wishes to make a case against the impossibility of their being 'infallible utterances', the baffling Hegelian logic is wheeled out once more. It is something to which Küng is deeply attached, for he had already stated it in a much earlier book: 'It is an over-simplication of truth to suppose that every proposition must be unambiguously true *or* false. Every proposition can, as far as the verbal formulation goes, be true *and* false according to how it is aimed, situated, intended' (*The Living Church*, 1963, p. 312). It would be useful if a theologian skilled in linguistic philosophy gave us a full account of Küng's linguistic ambiguities.

Another major unresolved difficulty concerns whether the concept of 'indefectibility' really is an adequate substitute for 'infallibility'. On this we cannot do better than quote a little fable of Dr E. J. Yarnold S.J., a member of the Oxford Theological Faculty:

The day before a contest a boxer met a fairy who promised him that he would be indefectible ... An encouraging promise, but how much could he count on? That he would win every round? That he would be leading on points at the end of the fight? Or simply that he would still be on his feet at the end of the fight?

I think it fair to say that similar ambiguities arise in Küng's appeal to the concept of indefectibility. Will the Church simply avoid being knocked out by error? Will it be more in truth than in error at the end of the world? Will it be totally free from error at the end of the world? Or will it soon correct any error as it occurs?

('Küng Examined', in *The Month*, September 1971, p. 78).

These are serious questions which still remain unresolved.

This excursus was designed not to 'refute' Küng (these are only two aspects of a vast question), but simply to illustrate that Catholic theologians were already engaged on the task of critically winnowing his ideas. But it never occurred to any serious theologian to say that 'Küng is no longer a Catholic theologian'. That is not part of theological discourse.

On one point, however, Küng is right beyond any shadow of doubt: some kind of restatement of the infallibility doctrine is absolutely required if ecumenism is to make any further progress. Küng's contribution may not be the right answer, but the right answer is to be sought somewhere along his lines – or it is to be found nowhere. 'Infallibility' is one of the three remaining obstacles in the Roman Catholic/Anglican dialogue. It will be an equally important problem in the dialogue with the Orthodox Churches which entered a new phase with the setting up of a joint Orthodox Roman Catholic Theological Commission (announced 30 November 1979). Since this dialogue with the Orthodox Churches is one of the main priorities of the pontificate of Pope John Paul II, help from any source (including Hans Küng) will be needed to suggest ways in which the deadlock over infallibility may be broken. Otherwise this bold ecumenical venture will fail.

Another of the ironies of this ironic tale is that when Pope John Paul II spoke in the Greek Cathedral of St George in Constantinople (Istanbul) on 30 November 1979, he was careful to describe his own papal office in terms which would not give offence to the Orthodox. Peter, he pointed out, was the 'chorus leader of the apostles' (a phrase borrowed from the Orthodox liturgy, where Peter is usually linked with Paul). Peter was said to have been entrusted with the task of 'ensuring the harmony of apostolic faith', a reassuringly 'Greek' expression which might leave room for Küng's 'indefectibility' but does not sit easily with Vatican I's 'infallibility'. In the same address John Paul quoted Acts 15:28 on 'not imposing what is not necessary', which is a perfect epitome of 'minimalism'. If infallibility turns out to be one of the post-schism definitions which are not to be imposed on the Orthodox – and they will never accept it in its Vatican I form – it seems unwise to reject a theologian who has provided a way of doing this with honour. What is likely is that the ban on Hans Küng as a Catholic theologian will remain, while a modified and 'disinfected' version of his ideas will be actually used in the dialogue with the Orthodox (and perhaps with the Anglicans).

But passions were running so high on the evening of 18 December 1979 that no one sought to defend Küng along these lines. For there was another feature of the Küng case which made his fate far worse than that of Schillebeeckx. Schillebeeckx, as we have seen, was defended by his 'Ordinary', Cardinal Jo Willebrands, admittedly at the eleventh hour but also handsomely and without any hedging reservations. The President of the German Bishops' Conference, Cardinal Joseph Höffner, had not only known what was going on all along, but had taken part in a secret meeting with Archbishop Jérôme Hamer in Brussels at which the final dispositions were made (cf. Ludwig Kaufmann S.J., in *Orientierung*, 15 January 1980, p. 4). The 18 December declaration of the German bishops endorsed the conclusions of the CDF. It echoed the CDF declaration in every respect, and added only a few more melancholy details. It mentioned that a conversation between Küng and representatives of the German bishops, 'lasting several hours in Stuttgart on 22 January 1977', had led to nothing. And it drew the practical conclusion that 'the appropriate diocesan Ordinary, Dr Georg Moser, will inform the Education Minister of the state of Baden-Württemberg, that the conditions for the *nihil obstat* no longer exist, and that Professor Küng has forfeited the canonical mission granted him when he was called to the University of Tübingen nineteen years ago' (cf. Appendix 3). The CDF and the German bishops had acted in concert. There were no loopholes.

Küng's immediate response, that Tuesday evening, 18 December, was that he would battle on. He learned of his condemnation only when he returned to Tübingen from Switzerland that morning. 'As a Catholic theologian', he said, 'I will continue to fight for Catholics and will not give in until this decision has been revoked.' He claimed widespread support among clergy and laity as well as among theologians. 'It is scandalous', he went on, 'that such inquisitorial procedures should take place in the twentieth century in a Church which has Jesus Christ as its foundation and which joins in the movement for human rights.' He concluded bleakly: 'I feel ashamed of my Church and very sad that the German cardinals and bishops should have collaborated in this inquisition.'

The next day, 19 December, proved that Küng was not mistaken in supposing that he would find much support among German Catholics. His Canon Law colleague in Tübingen, Professor Norbert Greinacher, quickly set up a 'Committee for the Defence of Christian Rights within the Church'. Among the immediate signatories were Johann Baptist Metz, Walter Dirks and Professor Walter Jens (also of Tübingen). Jens explained the reasons for their action. 'If the Church really wants to control theology in this way', he said, 'then theological faculties will have to leave the university.' Conversation between theologians and pastors ought to be 'free, fraternal and open'. 'From this point of view', he concluded, 'the Church under John XXIII was infinitely better off than it is today.' Küng lectured as usual, to a large and particularly attentive group of students, but he made no mention of what was on everyone's mind.

But later that same day, Küng had a two and a half hour conversation with his local Ordinary, 56-year-old Georg Moser, Bishop of Rottenburg-Stuttgart. Moser was well aware of the pastoral consequences for his diocese of the condemnation of Küng. The Höffner statement of the previous day had suggested that he would be a mere executant, who would faithfully carry out the orders he had received, dismiss Küng, and write a letter in this sense to the Minister of Education for the *Land*, the Christian Democrat Helmut Engler. This was not, however, how Moser conceived his role. He believed that it was his duty, as diocesan bishop, to work for reconciliation even though the declaration of the CDF was peremptory and admitted of no appeal. He later wrote: 'I had made up my mind what I had in conscience to do ... and that was understood in Rome.'

His conscience prompted him to try one last intervention, if possible with the Pope, whom he knew from working with *Pax Christi*, the Catholic peace movement. His conversations with Küng gave him sufficient grounds for believing that the theologian could produce a brief text which would at least serve as the basis for further discussion. Küng rapidly wrote the statement given as Appendix 4. That was on 20 December. The next day Moser went to Rome. Throughout Saturday, 22 December Moser tried in vain to get an audience with Pope John Paul, but he could not be fitted in. But his mission succeeded to the extent that it was agreed that a top-level meeting would take place as soon as possible after Christmas, and Friday, 28 December was the date settled on. This was a minor victory for Moser. It was less of a victory for Küng, who had hoped for a personal meeting with John Paul – a desire which Cardinal Höffner described as 'an expression of exaggerated self-importance'. But hope briefly flickered. Normally the Holy Office – the old name is appropriate here – took centuries to revise a verdict. Now it was prepared to re-open a question within two weeks. That such a meeting took place at all was a tribute to John Paul's readiness to look for solutions outside the framework of the ordinary procedure.

Meanwhile, and despite the Christmas festivities which were the worst possible time for organizing collective action, there was uproar in the diocese of Rottenburg-Stuttgart. The Committee for the Defence of Christian Rights in the Church now claimed 'several hundred' members. Teachers of religion in the diocese, clerical and lay, resigned their 'canonical mission' out of solidarity with Küng. A number of parish priests refused to preach Christmas sermons for the same reason: they would have felt fraudulent. And as in the Schillebeeckx case, but with so much less forewarning, the protests became international. Fifty Spanish theologians wrote to the newspaper *El Pais*. They interpreted the condemnation of Küng as 'an attack on the spirit and the logical development of Vatican II'. They wished to register their 'respectful but vigorous protest against the methods employed to silence Küng', and said that he should have been offered 'a final chance to reconsider his position on the disputed points, with a proper warning about what would happen if he reaffirmed them'. In the United States Leonard Swidler, editor of *Ecumenical Studies*, Charles E. Curran of the Catholic University, Washington, and David W. Tracy of the University of Chicago Divinity School, hastily put together a statement, promptly signed by seventy prominent Catholic theologians and lay people.

It said: 'We, as concerned and committed Roman Catholic theologians, cognizant that no one of us necessarily agrees with the opinions on particular issues of any other Roman Catholic scholar including Hans Küng, publicly affirm our recognition that Hans Küng is indeed a Roman Catholic theologian' (*National Catholic Reporter*, 28 December 1979). It was an oddly cold-waterish statement: no one necessarily agreed with Küng, but they were prepared to die – or at least to sign their names – for his right to say what he had to say.

But Küng's 'last chance', the direct appeal to the Pope, came about not as a response to the pressure of public opinion: it was the direct result of the intervention of Bishop Moser. He had convinced himself, the German bishops and the Pope, that Küng had said enough to reverse the earlier decision. Thus we arrive at the meeting at Castelgandolfo, where John Paul was taking a brief break, on Friday 28 December. The German 'delegation' (who had 'delegated' it?) was made up of Cardinals Joseph Höffner, Joseph Ratzinger, and Hermann Volk, together with Archbishop Otto Seier of Freiburg-im-Bresgau, the Metropolitan, and Moser himself. The meeting began at six o'clock in the evening. The Vatican was represented by Pope John Paul, who contented himself with listening, Cardinal Agostino Casaroli, Secretary of

State, Cardinal Franjo Seper, Prefect of the CDF, and Archbishop Jérôme Hamer O.P., its Secretary. The discussion continued over dinner and was not concluded until 11 p.m. A statement was promised for the following day, but it did not come. Evidently, there had been some difficulty in drawing it up and getting it agreed.

It came, eventually, on Sunday, 30 December. Its content was bleak. Moser's hopes had proved unfounded. It said that Küng had not conceded enough to get the ban rescinded. 'A thorough examination of the latest statement of Professor Küng', it said, 'led all those present to the conclusion that unfortunately there were insufficient grounds to change the decision made on 15 December' (text in Appendix 5). So in a sense Küng was now worse off than before. He had all along complained about the lack of any right of appeal against the decisions of the CDF. Now a form of appeal had been devised, against all expectations and precedents, and it had been rejected – with remarkable, not to say undue, haste, over dinner at Castelgandolfo on the Feast of the Holy Innocents.

However, the 30 December statement (which came from 'the Holy See'), while it changed nothing of substance, was noticeably milder in tone. It left the door half ajar for the future. It said: 'The Holy See and the German Episcopate have not given up the hope that Professor Küng – who has often declared his intention of remaining a Catholic theologian – will be moved after a period of reflection to take up an attitude which will permit his teaching mission to be restored.' It also noted that all those present – a distinguished company – were praying for Küng and said that they invited all men of good will to join with them. This was no doubt well-meant, but a theologian is obviously in a parlous state when all the leaders of the Church can do is to pray for him. In a further attempt to pour oil on by now distinctly troubled waters, the statement declared that the Küng decision in no way constituted 'a limitation of legitimate and necessary freedom of theological research' (though it unfortunately omitted to explain precisely why). And it also confidently stated that the decision did

94

not affect 'the attitude of the Church in its striving towards Christian Unity according to the principles of the Vatican II decree *On Ecumenism*'. This sounded rather like the politician's refuge of standing in the ocean and boldly declaring that his feet are not really wet. The ecumenical partners might be considered better judges of the effect of the condemnation: the World Council of Churches, which rarely comments on the 'internal affairs' of a Church, had said that it had done irreparable harm.

There was a suspicion that the top-level meeting and the appearance of an appeal procedure had been a sham, a charade, a belated attempt to recover lost ground. That evening Küng observed, more in sorrow than in anger:

I learned the result of the meeting in Rome with sorrow and without being able to understand it. The old maxim *audiatur altera pars* (let the other side be heard), is no longer respected in papal Rome. ... Evidently Rome cannot tolerate fraternal correction and loyal criticism. The rights of man and Christian charity are proclaimed to the world, but despite these fine words they are ignored within the Church itself ... Thanks to the Roman strategy, I remained merely an *object* and not a *partner* in the procedure. This conflict is not merely the Küng case: it concerns the Church itself which is on the way to squandering the chance to rebuild offered by the Second Vatican Council ... If I am not a Catholic theologian, I wonder how many priests and lay people can still call themselves Catholics. (*Frankfürter Rundschau*, 31 December 1979)

Bishop Moser, meanwhile, had continued to wrestle with his conscience. He communicated the official withdrawal of the canonical mission to Küng on 30 December, and also issued a public statement in which one could sense the pain and disappointment. Though he did not say so, it was clear that he had been urged to resign in protest. But he rejected this idea:

I can only say that a flight from responsibility, and a division of the diocese would be the worst of all solutions in this difficult time ... We are rather in the

95

position of a family that is going through a testing period. One thing is clear: running away is no answer. We must all try to stay as objective as possible, to master our emotions and not give up hope of reconciliation at some future date.

The New Year came. Pope John Paul preached doomladen, apocalyptic sermons at the Gesù on 31 December and in St Peter's on 1 January. Anti-christs were at work – among even the faithful. The world could be destroyed by an atomic war. The troubles of theologians seemed trivial in comparison with this cosmic battle. By 2 January Bishop Moser was sufficiently at peace with his conscience to be able to deliver the decisive letter to Helmut Engler, Minister of Education in the state of Baden-Württemberg, requesting Küng's removal and replacement.

This was more drastic than anyone had anticipated. Withdrawal of the faculty to teach 'as a Catholic theologian' was one thing: dismissal from the University of Tübingen was quite another. But Moser's letter was perfectly clear on the point. He summarized what had happened so far, with the two declarations of the CDF and Küng's unsuccessful appeal. He bit hard on the bullet and removed the last traces of ambiguity: 'I have made my own the decision of the CDF which has the approval of the Pope.' He then embarked upon an immensely complicated legal argument: 'In accordance with article 19 of the Imperial Concordat, with article 3 of the Bavarian Concordat, with article 12 of the Prussian Concordat and article 10 of the Baden Concordat, I am authorized to seek a replacement for Professor Dr Hans Küng.' The key legal point in the argument was that 'since the Faculty of Catholic Theology in the University of Tübingen has both *(zugleich)* a State and a Church status', the Church could legitimately call for the withdrawal of a Professor who has forfeited his 'canonical mission'.

There followed a legal tangle and a political battle of considerable complexity and asperity. Küng claimed that the decision involved 'an excessive interpretation' of

96

the various Concordats, and said that he would go to court if necessary to determine whether the Church was right to interpret them so broadly. He conceded that his permission to teach 'as a Catholic theologian' could be withdrawn, but not that he could be removed from the university. A spokesman for the Ministry of Education added fuel to the fire by saying that the meaning of the Concordat, devised in another age and for another purpose (a discreet way of alluding to the Nazi period), 'was not completely unambiguous'. He added that intensive negotiations were going on with the German bishops. Meanwhile the FDP (usually known abroad as the 'Liberals' and an ally of the SDP, the governing party) leapt on to the bandwagon and gave Küng the kind of support that cannot have done him much good. On 3 January 1980 the acting party chairman, Frau Liselotte Funcke, said that she found it 'thoroughly depressing' that an internationally recognized scholar should be excluded by the Church from a university chair. Her colleague, Hans-Dietrich Genscher, German Foreign Minister, expressed similar sentiments at a party meeting in Stuttgart on 6 January, the Feast of the Epiphany. Part of their motive was no doubt to embarrass Helmut Engler, a Christian Democrat and Minister of Education for the State of Baden-Württemberg. Mgr Joseph Homeyer, Secretary of the German Bishops' Conference, adopted a shocked tone and accused Frau Funcke of 'appalling ignorance' of the legal position, and on 7 January the Council of the Conference, 22 members, met in extraordinary session in Würzburg to decide what they ought to do about the crisis.

For by now crisis it was. On 6 January a group of students masqueraded in Dominican robes and burnt an effigy of Küng along with copies of his books, as a demonstration that the Holy Inquisition was back. This bizarre form of protest took place in the square outside Cologne cathedral and was intended to be in favour of Küng. The irony was lumpish indeed. Cardinal Joseph Ratzinger of Munich – thought by many Vatican-watchers to be likely to succeed Seper as Prefect of the CDF – preached a sermon in which he alleged that 'criticism of the papacy has reached a dramatic level' in the German Federal Republic. Pope John Paul II, he declared, 'has made the voice of the Church acceptable in a sceptical world'. Which was no doubt true. But as an editorial in the *Frankfürter Rundschau* pointed out: 'The removal of a theologian who has done more to bring back doubters to the Church than all the German bishops with their formal declarations, leaves one speechless and bitter' (31 December 1979).

Thus a move intended to confirm the faith of Catholic Christians had in many places the opposite effect: the attempt to settle doubts gave rise to new ones, and autocratic methods were revealed as clumsy and ineffectual.

The Küng case will continue to fester and rankle. Since Küng himself is not prepared to renounce his title of 'Catholic theologian', and since he is not alone in believing that this is justified, the next stage can only be one of continuing inner conflict within the Roman Catholic Church. No one intends to go into schism, since there are no grounds for it, and in any case it is an archaic idea given the pluralism of theology that has been recognized in the Church since Vatican II. The result is impasse and uneasiness. Neither Küng nor any of his supporters have the slightest desire to become 'Protestants'; and in any case it is difficulty to think of any Protestant Church that would welcome such rumbustious and awkward recruits. Their 'home', as Küng has so frequently said, is in the Roman Catholic Church. So they will hope to weather the storm, wait for a change of heart or a new pontificate, go underground, continue to publish and work for reform, convinced that they have a *droit de cité* in the Church as well-founded as that of anyone else. The concept of 'Her Majesty's loyal opposition' will gain ground. The number of 'fourth men' will grow (cf. Hebblethwaite, *The Runaway Church*, pp. 227–41: 'They can no more leave the Church than they can take leave of humanity. To do so would be a form of spiritual suicide').

There is one simple way of judging the effects of the Küng condemnation: it is to consider precisely who rejoiced in it. Foremost among them was Archbishop Marcel Lefebvre, leader of the Catholic traditionalists, who had come closer to schism than anyone else in the pontificate of Paul VI. He expressed his deep satisfaction at the withdrawal of Küng's canonical mission and was jubilant that 'the voice which for many years had taught doctrines which can scarcely be reconciled with constant Catholic teaching has now been silenced'. Küng, he declared, was 'an enemy of the faith' and, not to put too fine a point on it, a 'heretic' (a term which had been carefully avoided both by the CDF and the German bishops).

Hans Urs von Balthasar, a distinguished Swiss theologian, is a more substantial figure than Lefebvre. In his statement of approval for what had happened to Küng, he revealed how unhappy he had been with the pontificate of Paul VI: *204 998*

> John Paul II is safeguarding nothing less than the fundamental substance of Catholic faith. No one can deny that this was urgent after years of dogmatic, moral and liturgical permissiveness ... Perhaps it is inevitable that the Pope should give the impression of Hercules cleaning out the Augean stables.

The 'years of dogmatic, moral and liturgical permissiveness' can only refer to the pontificate of Paul VI. This is a monstrous calumny on the memory of a pope who, for all his scrupulous hesitancy, tried to govern the Church from the 'centre' and in complete faithfulness to the letter and spirit of Vatican II. And that a theologian should compare the work of his fellow theologians with the contents of the Augean stables marks a new low in theological controversy.

Fr Paul Crane S.J. is not a theologian. He is an English Jesuit who can sniff out heresy at a distance. He wrote a letter to *The Catholic Herald* commending Pope John Paul for what he had so wisely done. It concluded:

> Catholics can only thank God that Pope John Paul has begun so valiantly a task so long overdue. In his

prosecution of it, all but a tiny dissident minority within the Church will give him the support of their prayers.

Meanwhile they look to the bishops, in particular, to follow his example: to see to it that all those responsible for religious instruction on all levels within their dioceses respect the basic right to be given God's truth that belongs to each of the faithful. (4 January 1980) Again there is the emphasis on the failure of Paul VI ('a task so long overdue'). Equally sinister is the suggestion that a heresy-hunt should now be conducted ('on all levels') to weed out unsuspecting catechists, teachers, nuns, curates, anyone in fact who does not accept the extreme right-wing version of Catholicism propounded by a Crane. One may be reasonably sure that the CDF did not have this in mind when it sentenced Küng; one may be equally sure that such could be its effect.

In the hubbub of voices from those who rejoiced in the condemnation of Küng and those who protested against it, the voice of moderation passed almost unnoticed. It was less dramatic. It did not make the headlines. It began, indeed, to sound like the memory of another age. Yet it is essential to attend to it for the sake of the future of the Church. Cardinal Basil Hume represents the voice of moderation. He wrote an article in *The Times*. Though his theme was a Christian agenda for the next decade and though his main point was a denunciation of the wastefulness and injustice of the arms race, he could not refrain from comment on the controversial issue. Two carefully composed paragraphs summed up his position:

Recent controversy concerning prominent theologians in the Roman Catholic Church has disquieted many and raised in some minds doubts about the future of ecumenical dialogue. We have a problem. How do we reconcile the right and duty of the theologian to pursue his researches in academic freedom with the limitations of the human mind to discover truths about God which always lie beyond its competence? The responsibility of the teaching authority within the Church to safeguard the authentic teaching of the Christian

Gospel has to be maintained; and at the same time the duty of the theologian to speculate has to be asserted. From time to time the two will clash; better this than indifference and apathy.

It is legitimate to argue over whether it is better for all concerned that investigations into a theologian's orthodoxy should be conducted in secrecy or publicly. There are strong arguments for each practice. Theologians and the Sacred Congregation need not be in conflict. Both are needed to ensure that, on the one hand, fundamental truths are protected and, on the other, that the academic freedom of the theologian be recognized to pursue his studies and to draw out the consequences of his belief according to the best principles of scholarly integrity. The co-operation of both is the best guarantor of a living faith within the Church and is our indispensable contribution to the ecumenical dialogue. The pilgrim Church needs some infallible signposts.   (*The Times*, 3 January 1980)

It may all seem rather tortuous. But to admit that 'we have a problem' is itself a significant step forward. Again, Cardinal Hume rejects any solution to the problem which involves the suppression of one of its elements, viz the duty of the theologian 'to speculate'. (Perhaps a better word could have been chosen, for 'speculate' suggests an ivory tower approach.) Moreover the recognition that from time to time the two will clash is interpreted *positively* by Cardinal Hume: if this did not happen theology would be dead. On the question of whether the investigation of theological opinions should be pursued in public or in private, Cardinal Hume professes himself agnostic: 'There are strong arguments for each practice.' That is a more critical remark than it may appear; for the current orthodoxy is that all the arguments favour secrecy. Since Cardinal Hume is President of the European Bishops' Assembly, his views carry extra weight.

One does not expect a rebellion of cardinals and bishops. But one does expect them to make – respectfully and collegially – representations to Pope John Paul. For, as all the quotations in the last part of this chapter have indicated, Pope John Paul is involved in the procedures that have taken place. They cannot be attributed merely to the enterprise of subordinates in the CDF. They are the result of a conscious decision. We therefore have no option but to examine John Paul's general views on theology to determine whether what we are witnessing is likely to be a temporary and limited campaign or a policy that will mark the whole pontificate. The stakes are high.

6. *John Paul II and Theology*

> Let there be no mistake, his whole past shows that he
> will be prepared to swing those Keys of Peter to devas-
> tating effect should he deem it necessary.
>
> > – an anonymous Vatican 'source', quoted in
> > James Oram, *The People's Pope*

There is a natural reluctance on the part of Catholics
to criticize a reigning pope. Dead popes are a different
matter. So while right-wing Catholics danced merry jigs
on what they thought was the tomb of Hans Küng – and
it was only a matter of time before Schillebeeckx would
follow him into the grave – 'liberal' Catholics were placed
in a quandary. They sought refuge in various consoling
strategies, the chief of which was to try to drive a wedge
between Pope John Paul II and the Congregation for the
Doctrine of Faith. Nowhere was this better exemplified
than in a grave and worried leading article in *The Tablet*.
It explained:

> The moves against Professors Schillebeeckx and Küng
> were in train long before he [Karol Wojtyla] became
> Pope. So far the action has not been *motu proprio*. It
> is not generally recognized that where the Pope
> authorizes a curial document this is not necessarily a
> sign that he is fully engaged with it. (5 January 1980,
> p. 3)

But this was whistling in the dark. There was no evidence
that John Paul was not fully committed to the actions of
the CDF, and a certain amount of evidence that he
actually was. Wishful thinking could not alter this fact.

By January 1980 there were sufficient indications that
the new pontificate would be one of restoration and reaction. The relatively liberal policy on laicizations, which
meant that priests could resign without fuss or dishonour
and continue to serve the Church in some useful capacity,

was abandoned without any consultation. The Special Synod of the Netherlands Province of the Roman Catholic Church (to give it its full title) met in Rome on 14 January 1980: it was an undisguised attempt to restore lost discipline in what the Vatican regarded as an unruly and dissident Church. Nuns were told to return to their habits and to prayer. The Jesuits were warned not to succumb to the temptations of secularization; and priests like William Callahan S.J., who had been advocating the ordination of women, were privately told by Fr Pedro Arrupe, the General of the Jesuits, to desist – this question was not on the agenda of the pontificate.

Most crucially of all, the Second Vatican Council, though it continued to be honoured and quoted extensively, was given an interpretation that was narrow, restrictive and, in the end, thoroughly distorting. In his address to the US bishops gathered in Chicago on 5 October, John Paul quoted John XXIII who in his opening speech to the Council on 11 October 1962 had said: 'The greatest concern of the Ecumenical Council is this: that the sacred deposit of Christian doctrine should be more effectively guarded and taught' (*The Documents of Vatican II*, ed. Walter Abbott S.J., Chapman, 1966, p. 713). But that was not all that John XXIII had said. He did not have a predominantly defensive outlook. He did not believe that the task of the Council was merely to re-assert the age-old doctrine of the Church. 'For this, a Council was not necessary', he remarked (ibid., p. 715). The real point of the Council, he went on, was to take

a step forward towards a doctrinal penetration and a formation of the consciousness of the faithful in perfect conformity to the authentic doctrine which, however, should be studied and expounded through the methods of research and the literary forms of modern thought. The substance of the ancient deposit of faith is one thing, and the way it is presented is another. (ibid., p. 715)

This distinction between 'substance' and 'form' had provided the charter for conciliar and post-conciliar theology. John Paul omits this passage from his canon of the Council, and elects to lay the emphasis on 'guarding and teaching' Christian doctrine. Theologians, meanwhile, had been working on quite different premises. Clash was inevitable.

Two other features of the pontificate confirmed this judgement. There had been another shift in the Vatican's flexible power structure. While Paul VI had concentrated authority in the Secretariat of State, so that he could keep a firm grip on everything that was going on, John Paul II has restored the relative autonomy of the Congregation for the Doctrine of Faith. The difference this makes is that the Secretariat of State, though it might not be theologically well-informed, at least had some inkling of 'diplomatic' consequences, a knowledge of the effect of public opinion and a sense of timing. The CDF, on the other hand, zealously defends 'orthodoxy' with single-minded intensity and a complete disregard for the consequences. This chimes in neatly with the 'populist' approach of John Paul II. He has frequently appealed to the masses over the heads of the few malcontents who are, it is said, rocking Peter's Barque. In the same way the CDF repeatedly argues that 'the people of God' have the right to receive sound and authentic doctrine, without being sold short. The rights of theologians are reduced to 'the right not to be misunderstood'. In case of conflict, the right of the faithful as a whole takes precedence.

The new policy towards theologians fits in with another characteristic of Pope John Paul. He likes to tackle problems head-on. He does not beat about the bush. Where Paul VI was cautious, dilatory, diplomatic and reluctant to provoke an open break, John Paul II charges dashingly ahead like the Polish cavalry, in pursuit of his vision of a Church in which order will have been restored. At the Vatican Council, Paul VI always sought for compromise which meant that, as he put it, there would be *pas de vaincus, mais des convaincus* (no vanquished, but only the convinced). John Paul II does not seem to mind if the battlefield is strewn with the corpses of fallen theologians. Though apologists point out that all the processes which came to fruition in his pontificate had already been started under Paul VI, that merely emphasizes the difference: for Paul VI may have allowed the CDF to start proceedings, but none were ever concluded. Under John Paul II the tempo has been speeded up, the workload increased, and there are no inhibitions about concluding. These differences depend partly on temperament and partly on previous convictions.

So it will be useful to investigate the attitude of Karol Wojtyla to theologians *before* he became pope. This evidence will not of itself be absolutely decisive, for a man can and frequently does change on becoming pope. But if, as we shall find, there is perfect coherence between before and after, then we shall know that we are right to stress the personal factor. It would be ironical if theologians who are said to have placed their own 'personal convictions' above the doctrine of the Church are in fact being judged from the standpoint of another set of 'personal convictions'. The difference is that the second set of convictions are now embodied in the man who became pope.

No great sleuth-like qualities are needed to discover what Cardinal Karol Wojtyla thought about theologians. His views on the subject were clear and oft-repeated (the question has been studied in great detail by Henryk Nowacki, *'La Teologia nella Chiesa postconciliare'*, in *Studia in Honorem Caroli Wojtyla*, a special number of *Angelicum*, vol. 56, 1979, pp. 239–60). In 1971 he gave an address to the Polish Congress of Theology on the theme 'Theology and Theologians in the post-conciliar Church' (*Teologia i theologowie w Kosciele Posoborowym*. Cf. Robert Modras' presentation of this text in *Commonweal*, 14 September 1979, pp. 493–5).

What is interesting and curious about his treatment is that the entire lecture is taken up with the question of the relationship between theologians and the *magisterium*. Now there are many other questions that merit discussion when one is speaking of theology, and most theologians do not spend much time worrying about their relationship to the *magisterium*. They live and move and have their being within the tradition of the Church; and the relationship to the *magisterium* only becomes a live question when there are difficulties with it. But for Cardinal Wojtyla, even already in 1971, this was *the* central question. It obsessed him. The Council, he explained, had been the model of fruitful collaboration between theologians and bishops. But it was long over. And since then the relationship had been soured. The proper task of theologians, he said, was to 'guard, defend and teach the sacred deposit of revelation' in close association with the bishops but in strict subordination to them. The function of theologians is 'purely consultative' (Roman jargon for saying they may not 'decide' anything), and he quoted with approval a remark of Cardinal Franjo Seper, already Prefect of the CDF, who had warned against 'making the Word of God an instrument for forcing one's own opinions'.

Theologians and scholars should not be allowed to usurp the teaching function in the Church. It belongs uniquely to the Pope and the bishops. Now there would have been no reason to stress all this unless something had gone wrong. Wojtyla believed that certain theologians, whom he did not propose to name, were responsible for sowing seeds of doubt in the minds of the faithful on such fundamental doctrines as christology, the Trinity, the real presence of Christ in the Eucharist, and the indissolubility of marriage. It may be possible to question some of the traditional formulations of faith, but never at the expense of the substance of revealed and defined truth which is unchanging. He maintained that post-conciliar theologians had not always respected this principle. They had succumbed to pressures from outside the Church which had led them into 'false irenicism', 'humanism' and even 'secularism'.

Happily, he noted, Poland was on the whole free from such disastrous tendencies. With a touch of resentment, he referred to 'certain circles, especially in the West', which regarded Polish theology as 'conservative'. This he rejected by making a distinction between a mere clinging to the past and 'an honest relationship to the deposit of faith and respect for the *magisterium*'. Because of the barrier of language, Poland imported more theology than it exported, and Wojtyla was not happy about this imbalance.

None of these ideas were particularly original. They provided a slightly milder version of themes frequently rehearsed more bluntly by Cardinal Stefan Wyszynski, Primate of Poland. He held the view that modern theologians – particularly the group associated with the multi-language review *Concilium* – had emptied the churches in the West and ought not to be allowed to do the same in Poland. 'We want a Polish theology for Poland', he told the 1972 Congress of Theology, 'written from the standpoint of the East for a community living in the East.' But in effect, as some Polish theologians were not slow to point out, the call for a 'Polish theology' meant in practice the rejection of Western theology and a tight rein on Polish theological experiment – justified on the political grounds that in a communist country there must be no hint of divisions within the Church, for the government would at once intervene to deepen and exploit them. 'Polish theology', then, was coloured by the Polish situation. It was not an autonomous intellectual activity. It was at the service of the Church's unity, narrowly conceived, in an embattled situation. The result was a curious parallel between the way in which the Polish Communists rejected foreign influences such as Euro-communism as threatening, and the way in which the Polish bishops rejected foreign influences such as the Dutch *New Catechism* also as threatening. But each wanted for the other what it refused for itself.

It is hardly surprising that the Polish theological scene was rather unexciting. This was the judgement of Fr Andrzej Zuberbier who wrote in 1974:

Polish theology flows quietly by, some might say monotonously by. There are no problems, no conflicts of views, no noisy proclamations. If a discussion takes place at all, it happens within the narrow circle of the involved. Theology does not have the function which it has in the West, where it is critical of the whole activity of the Church.

('What Polish Theology is Like', *Wiez*, December 1974)

Another Polish theologian, Tadeusz Silkorski, remarked that 'Polish theologians always appear on the battlefield after the battle is over'. An obsession with 'safety' keeps them at a safe distance from all controversy, and yet, he adds nostalgically, 'it is in these dialectical clashes that truth is being born' ('Feast of Polish Theology', *Collectanea Theologica*, No. 2, 1977). Polish theologians generally had come to believe that 'Polish theology' could not be content with being merely 'anti-Western'. By 1978 – the last Congress at which Cardinal Wojtyla was present – Zuberbier had begun to argue that Polish theologians should make themselves familiar with the riches of the Orthodox tradition, and in this way they would begin to fulfil their vocation as Slavs brought up in the Latin tradition, and so make a unique contribution to theological thought and ecumenism. Cardinal Wojtyla enthusiastically endorsed this idea, suggested that Polish theologians were much better prepared for this task than Western theologians, and thought that it would contribute to a reasonable 'division of labour' among theologians in Europe. But this remains an aspiration rather than an achievement.

There was little in the theological output of the 1970s calculated to change the views which Wojtyla had already expressed in 1971. Indeed, if anything, the major works of the 1970s such as Schillebeeckx's *Jesus – An Experiment in Christology* (1974) and Hans Küng's *On Being A Christian* (also 1974) represented an even greater threat to someone holding the views he did. For they dealt with the central mystery of Christianity, the nature of Christ himself. But there is not much evidence that Wojtyla, during this period, was closely following theological literature. He was a busy diocesan bishop and when he burned the midnight oil, his reading was mostly in philosophy and ethical philosophy, as a glance at the footnotes of *The Acting Person* (*The Yearbook of Phenomenological Re-*

search, D. Reidel, 1979) will show. Strictly theological questions did not engage his attention. The bibliography given in the special number of *Angelicum* lists only eighteen 'theological articles' between 1950 and 1978; and this includes two articles in *Osservatore Romano* and an article on 'St Joseph' in *Tygodnik Powszechny*, the Kraków Catholic weekly paper. The remaining articles were mostly commentaries on conciliar texts. None of them tackled a major theological problem. It was clear that Cardinal Wojtyla did not consider himself to be a professional theologian. His real academic work was in ethical philosophy. This was confirmed by Fr Mieczyslaw Malinski, author of a book called *Pope John Paul: The Life of My Friend Karol Wojtyla* (1979). He said on Swiss Television (23 December 1979) that he could affirm 'with certainty' that John Paul had never read a book by Küng so long as he was in Kraków. 'He was in no way a theologian', he added.

Nevertheless Cardinal Wojtyla continued to be interested in theological divagations. In 1977 Paul VI paid him the honour – rare for a non-Roman – of an invitation to preach the Lenten retreat for himself and the Curia. The following passage forms part of Wojtyla's 'Conclusion' and illustrates the meaning of the title of the book containing the text of his meditations: *Sign of Contradiction*. To understand this passage, one needs to recall the usage which distinguishes the 'first world' (the developed West) from the 'second world' (the communist regimes) and the 'third world' (countries that are developing). Cardinal Wojtyla was speaking of the 'first world':

Certainly there is in this world a powerful reserve of faith, and also a considerable margin of freedom for the Church's mission. But often it is no more than a margin. One need only take note of the principal tendencies governing the means of social communication, one need only pay heed to what is passed over in silence and what is shouted aloud, one need only lend an ear to what encounters most opposition, to perceive that where Christ is accepted there is at the same time an opposition to the full truth of his Person, his mission and the Gospel. There is a desire to 're-shape' him, to adapt him to suit mankind in this era of progress and to make him fit in with the programme of modern civilization –which is a programme of consumerism and not of transcendental ends. There is opposition to him from those standpoints, and the truth proclaimed and recorded in his name is not tolerated (cf Acts 4: 10, 12, 18). This opposition to Christ which goes hand in hand with paying him lip service – and it is found among those who call themselves his disciples – is particularly symptomatic of our times.

(Sign of Contradiction 1979, p. 199)

What did the curial Cardinals make of this? What did Cardinal Seper think? The passage was not altogether clear. It makes you fairly bursting to fight (as Raymond Mortimer once said of the style of Bernanos), but it doesn't show you the enemy. It is written in a sort of code. Let us crack the code. The passage breaks down into four propositions. 1) The Western world, sometimes known as the 'free world', gives Christians a certain freedom, but at the same time imposes on them its false values. It is characterized by 'consumerism' – a term which Wojtyla uses to mean not being a wise and prudent consumer (à la Ralph Nader) but a heedless consumer. If the Western world has other values – a concern for democracy and freedom of speech, for instance – they are not his concern. 2) The mass media play an important part in the process of instilling false values; and therefore one should not be surprised if they go chasing after spurious novelties in theology. To have public opinion on one's side is not necessarily an advantage. 3) Christ is refashioned according to these false values, and therefore 4) many who call themselves Christians are frauds or hypocrites.

As an account of the Western world it does seem rather inadequate. One wonders on what experience or experiences it is based. Certainly no theologian working on christology would recognize himself in this depressing portrait.

Yet it is precisely this 'perception' of the Western world that colours the theological judgements of John Paul II. He has persuaded himself that Western theologians have succumbed to consumerism and distorted the image of Christ to turn him into a 'modern progressive'. Moreover this curious view of the West is accompanied by an apocalyptic vision which gives added urgency and drama to his pontificate. For example, at the end of his sermon at Santa Maria Maggiore on 8 December 1979, he suddenly 'revealed' that, at their meeting early in November, the College of Cardinals had expressed a desire to entrust themselves and the whole Church to the protection of Mary the Mother of God. He did not explain who had made this suggestion or how it came about. It had never been mentioned before. John Paul, at any rate, said that he had welcomed the idea with enthusiasm for the following reason:

I myself feel a profound need to be obedient to the invitation explicit in the *proto-evangelion* [a term used for Genesis 3:15: 'I will put enmity between thee and the woman, and between thy seed and her seed; it shall bruise thy head and thou shalt bruise its heel'].

In this *difficult age of ours* are we not witnesses of this 'enmity'? What else can we do, what else can we desire, other than to be still more closely united to Christ, to the Son of the Woman?

(Italics in the *Osservatore Romano* text, 10–11 December 1979, p. 2).

Here even experienced code-crackers tend to give up. But clearly John Paul thinks that the times are awry, that a crisis is impending, that the cosmic battle between Good and Evil is entering a new and decisive phase. It is relevant to recall that in the pre-conclave period in October 1978, the right wing used what is known in Italy as 'the strategy of tension'. That is, they stressed that some vague cataclysm was looming (a 'third world war' according to Vatican demonologist, Corrado Balducci, in *Osservatore Romano*) and that therefore a strong pope was needed to stand in the breach and defy the forces of evil. If this is how Pope John Paul pictures himself, then obviously he will not have much time for distracting theologians. The time of the apocalypse does not allow for hesitations and scruples.

Having sketched the 'theological horizon' out of which John Paul speaks, we now come to an address in which there was an almost direct reference to the Schillebeeckx case. On 26 October he spoke to the thirty members of the International Theological Commission (ITC). Their annual session had been devoted to christology and in particular to an examination of various 'non-Chalcedonian christologies'. The Pope was speaking, moreover, just about a week after Schillebeeckx gave his first tell-all interview to Richard Auwerda (in *De Volkskrant*, 18 October 1979).

The ITC had been set up by Pope Paul VI in 1969 as a way of continuing the harmonious collaboration between theologians and the *magisterium* that had proved so successful during the Second Vatican Council. The real makers of the Council had been French and German theologians like Yves Congar, Henri de Lubac and Karl Rahner, with notable contributions from Louvain in Belgium and Nijmegen in Holland (including Schillebeeckx). So true was this that a right-wing critic, Fr Ralph Wiltgen, wrote a polemical book, engagingly called *The Rhine Flows into the Tiber*, in which he developed the thesis that the Council had been a conspiracy of 'Rhineland theologians' who contrived to pull wool over the eyes of the bishops. Paul VI did not see things that way. The point of the ITC was that the expertise of these extra-urban theologians should continue to be available for the service of the *magisterium*. For in the past, the theological advisers of the pope had been largely drawn from the Roman universities, and in the main they represented a narrower view of theology than was found elsewhere. Their contribution to the Council was minimal. They were largely objicients to what others proposed. The ITC would be able to provide a better balance of theological advice. Schillebeeckx, by the way, was never a member of the ITC. Though the Dutch bishops had put forward his name, his candidacy was never accepted.

The ITC, then, was a bright and shining new post-conciliar organism, with the admirable purpose of delivering the pope from Roman narrowness. It was another way in which – and this language was often used – 'the periphery would be permanently present at the centre'. Since, moreover, Roman theological advice to the pope had come traditionally through the mediation of the CDF, the very existence of the ITC was a blow and a threat to the CDF. No longer 'supreme', it had a counterweight, and a powerful one. This cannot be excluded as a surreptitious factor in the events we have been describing. *Odium theologicum* is more tenacious and unforgiving than other forms of hatred: celibacy carries with it both a greater dedication and a more relentless concentration on the pursuit of error and the defence of orthodoxy. There is no one to tell a Roman official that he is taking himself too seriously.

From what we already know of John Paul II, he could be expected to enhance the CDF and to downgrade the ITC. The process had already begun. The ITC's advice was increasingly ignored. Karl Rahner resigned from it in 1974 on the grounds, he claimed, of 'old age' but chiefly because it was 'stewing in its own juice'. 'It sets itself problems,' he said in an interview, 'speaks about them in a more or less praiseworthy way, but then nothing happens' (*Herder Korrespondenz*, February 1974). In other words, the ITC was becoming 'domesticated', integrated into the system. It was an instance of 'tokenism' which left the theological scene still dominated, as before, by the Roman universities (and especially by the Dominican Angelicum and the Jesuit Gregorian). It could be described as an ineffectual safety-valve. This is unfair to the thirty distinguished theologians who belong to it, but they are trapped in a situation not of their making. They confer almost entirely by correspondence and meet in plenary session only once a year.

Their 1979 plenary session was concluded on 26 October. It took on a special significance since their theme had been christology. The veil of secrecy hangs over their meeting. But enough is known of their proceedings to say that they had examined various 'non-Chalcedonian christologies' and not rejected them outright. In particular they had studied the christologies of Schillebeeckx and Küng. Unlike Fr Jean Galot S.J., they did not take the view that 'non-Chalcedonian christologies' are by definition erroneous and heretical, and they were sympathetic towards attempts to express in contemporary language the essential faith of the Church. One paper, for example, was concerned with 'Spirit-christology', that is, the possibility that the mission and nature of Jesus can be better understood by saying that he was 'uniquely filled with the Holy Spirit' than by taking the *Logos* or Word as their starting-point. This was very close to the Schillebeeckx and Küng position.

For all these reasons, John Paul's address at the conclusion of their meeting was no mere formality, and it was awaited with considerable interest. He did not disappoint. He tackled the controversial questions directly, and made his own position translucently clear (Latin is a language designed for clarity). He made some preliminary flattering remarks about his esteem for the ITC and his high expectations of it. Then came a reminder that they must behave 'responsibly'. Had they not? He said that though they 'participated in the *magisterium*', they only participated in it *'to some extent'*. He wished to stress this phrase. He neatly quoted his predecessor, Paul VI, who had remarked that only the authentic *magisterium* was of divine origin, and that it alone possessed 'the charism of truth, which could not be communicated to others, and for which there was no substitute'. (For Paul VI, cf. *Acta Apostolicae Sedis*, 65, 1973, p. 557.) The role of the ITC was, therefore, clearly subservient. But it was a little difficult to see the point of this exhortation in an address to this particular group. There was no evidence that the ITC was on the point of some collective folly or proposing to set itself up as a rival *magisterium*. They mostly wanted to go home and get on with the new term which had already started.

John Paul II then turned to the central question:
We know that in this plenary session you have been

concerned with questions of christology and we hope that your work will be fruitful. We have already seen and read attentively the papers that have been prepared, dealing with historical and theological questions ... There are indeed new aspects of christology which may be brought to light and require a thorough investigation – always, however, in the light of truths contained in the source of revelation which throughout the centuries have been infallibly proclaimed by the *magisterium*.

'Infallibly proclaimed': so much for Küng. But a certain amount of cramped room for manoeuvre remained. John Paul then went on to give his own account of New Testament christology. The crucial differences with the Schillebeeckx account will leap to mind:

'You are the Christ, the Son of the Living God' (Matthew 16: 16). This is the witness explicitly borne by the Prince of the Apostles, illumined by grace and drawing upon his own experience. 'It is not flesh and blood that have revealed this to you, but my Father who is in heaven' (16: 17). These words provide as it were a summary of our whole faith. The christological faith, which the Catholic Church professes, is based, under the guidance of strengthening grace, on the experience of Peter, and of the rest of the apostles and disciples who knew Jesus personally, who touched the hands of the Word of life (cf. 1 John 1: 1). What they experienced in this way, they then interpreted in the light of the Passion and Resurrection and under the guidance (*ex motione*) of the Holy Spirit. From this grew the first 'synthesis' which is expressed in the professions of faith and the hymns of the apostolic letters.

Here I interrupt the Pope to have a dialogue with him. Three remarks seem appropriate. The first is that the concept of 'growth' or 'development' implied by the last sentence (*Exinde orta est*, says the Latin text) brings John Paul very close to Schillebeeckx and most modern scholarship. But there remains a question about 'how much growth?' Secondly, many scholars (especially Martin Hengel) have stressed that the christological formulas found in the Letters of St Paul are essentially liturgical expressions: the Church is most itself when it is at prayer. In that sense it would have been relevant to ask Schillebeeckx not 'What do you think?' but 'How do you pray?' John Paul's reference to the 'hymns of the apostolic letters' suggests that he has come close to grasping this point. Finally, his address acknowledges that it is through the early Christian communities and their faith that we can draw close to Christ. In these three ways, the gap between Schillebeeckx and John Paul II is narrowed. But it is not completely closed. For the Pope uses Matthew 16:16 as the key for his interpretation of later developments, while Schillebeeckx would want to maintain that since Matthew 16:16 itself is an interpretation, it cannot be used in this way.[1]

Having dealt with the New Testament, John Paul went on to speak about the contribution made by the Ecumenical Councils of the Church:

> In the course of time the Church, always reverting to this witness and re-experiencing its power, expressed its faith ever more precisely (*verbis semper accutioribus*) in the great Councils. As theologians of this Commission, you have studied these Councils, with special attention to Nicaea and Chalcedon. The formulations (*formulae*) of these ecumenical Councils have permanent validity (*vim habent permanentem*); however, the historical circumstances and the questions that were alive in the Church at that time and to which the Councils responded, should not be neglected.

This was the crux of the matter: but Schillebeeckx and Küng were not yet ruled out of court. They could claim that there was a difference of emphasis. They wished to

1. It is perhaps relevant to point out that Matthew 16:16 is not only the foundation of the faith of the Church; since these words are uttered by Peter, they can also be taken as saying something about the Petrine ministry. There can be no doubt that John Paul II makes this link: it was the main theme of the homily preached at his inauguration Mass on 22 October 1978. (Cf. *The Year of Three Popes*, p. 191 *et seq.*)

stress the time-bound, and therefore limited, nature of conciliar statements, whilst retaining 'what they intended to say'. John Paul II, on the other hand, starts from the universal validity of conciliar statements and then, only then, looks at their historical conditionings. The opposition though sharp is not unsurmountable, given good will on both sides. However, John Paul went on to stress the importance of adhering not merely to 'what was intended' but to the language in which it was expressed:

> The permanent validity of dogmatic formulations is made all the more clear from the fact that they use ordinary and familiar language, although from time to time (*interdum*) philosophical expressions occur. It follows from this that the *magisterium* does not follow any particular school [of philosophy], since it uses the expressions (*locutiones*) which are to hand in all human experience.

Again, it might be thought, the difference with Schillebeeckx is one of emphasis. John Paul stressed the ordinariness of the language used, and therefore its universal validity and availability; Schillebeeckx, on the other hand, had pointed to the technical philosophical language that was used (e.g. talk of 'person' and 'nature') and rested his case for 'interpretation' on this fact.

John Paul's treatment of christology ended there. But he went on to make a number of remarks which are relevant to the theological enterprise more generally:

> It is clear that the study of theology cannot be confined merely to repeating dogmatic formulations, but that it must help the Church towards an ever greater appreciation of the mystery of Christ. For the Saviour also speaks to the men of our time. The Second Vatican Council reminds us that 'Only in the mystery of the Incarnate Word does the mystery of man take on light'.
> (*Church in the World of Today*, No. 22)

On this point John Paul quoted his own encyclical, which was an expression of a profound Christian humanism:

> The man who wishes to understand himself thoroughly ... must draw near to Christ, with his unrest, uncer-

tainty and even his weakness and sinfulness, with his life and his death. He must, so to speak, enter into him with his whole self, he must 'appropriate' and assimilate the whole reality of the Incarnation and Redemption in order to find himself.

(*Redemptor Hominis*, No. 10)

Here John Paul was in harmony with contemporary theology. He had himself noted in his 1971 lecture that the shift from a cosmological approach to an anthropological and personalist approach was the most important achievement of Vatican II. In other words he wanted to say that revelation not only reveals God to man but at the same time and by the same token reveals man to man himself. It is an error to speak as though all the mystery were on the side of God and as though man were perfectly clear to himself. This was hinted at in *The Acting Person* and more fully developed in *Love and Responsibility*. It is the basis of his desire for a dialogue with the human sciences. It seems to leave room for a 'christology from below' provided, however, that the 'christology from below' attains and is fulfilled by a 'christology from on high'. There is space for dialogue here. But this is also the limit of John Paul's concessions to 'modernity', for he subordinates the human sciences to theological goals. It was the next point he made in his address to the ITC:

It happily comes about that the great majority of theologians, following the example of St Thomas Aquinas, believe that philosophy should be made to serve the purposes of faith. For every science is attached to its own principles and methods: so it is that theology judges all the questions that are submitted to it from the principles of faith. It would act against its own nature if it relied on principles drawn from elsewhere and assented to conclusions which could not be harmonized with its own principles.

So it would. But this harmony is not achieved at a stroke or by the metaphysical proclamation that it has been achieved. It is a hard-won conquest.

Finally, John Paul returned to what all along had been

119

his main theme: the relationship between theologians and the *magisterium*, and the possible 'difficulties' that might arise:

On this we want to stress that both the *magisterium* and theologians are bound by the same bonds, that they are subject to the Word of God, to the 'sense of faith' which in times past and today is alive and flourishes in the Church, to the documents of tradition in which the common faith is proposed to the people, and finally to the pastoral care and mission which both should have in view. If these points were attended to, difficulties which may perhaps occur would be more easily overcome. Moreover, theologians who teach their subject in places of higher education should always remember that they do not teach on their own authority but in virtue of the mission they have received from the Church.

There followed a reference to the apostolic constitution, *Sapientia Christiana*, which speaks of the 'canonical mission' (No. 27). So these were not merely theoretical considerations on the nature of theology: they prepared the ground for the disciplinary actions that would follow. They were a warning that any conflict or apparent conflict between theologians and the *magisterium* would be resolved in favour of the *magisterium*. They were a clear indication that no time lapse would be allowed in which theologians might break new ground, experiment, tackle fresh questions or make 'creative mistakes'. Pope John Paul had not changed his mind since his 1971 address to the Polish Congress of Theology. The task of a theologian is 'to guard, defend and teach the sacred deposit of revelation' in close association with the bishops and in strict subordination to them. The primary function of theology is apologetic.

There is one more address of John Paul II that is relevant to the theme of theologians and the *magisterium*. Its timing gave it a special interest. At six o'clock in the evening of 15 December, the very day on which Schillebeeckx had concluded his hearing, Pope John Paul went to the Gregorian University. Its crowded aula was decked out for the occasion with tapestries. There was another reason why the address was awaited with keen anticipation. On 21 September the Jesuits, who run the Gregorian, had been sharply criticized by the Pope. No very precise charges were uttered, but he had hinted darkly at the growing influence of 'secularization' and a lack of due fidelity to the *magisterium*. It hardly seemed likely that the Pope could contrive to deliver an address in which there would be no mention of the two controversies. But at first his listeners were disappointed. All was sweetness and light and reconciliation.

John Paul's praise for the Gregorian University, the genial creation of the fertile mind of St Ignatius, was unstinted. It had already provided the Church with 19 saints, 24 blessed, 16 popes and innumerable cardinals and bishops. Its professors had always been characterized, he noted, by a double commitment which was fundamental to all theological research – and ears began to prick up a little at this:

That of a loyal and docile openness to the suggestions of the *magisterium*, in conformity with the specific spirit of the Society of Jesus ... and of ever more attentiveness to the developing sciences which could have possible links with the study of theology.

The second point was developed a little more fully. The history of the Gregorian, said the Pope, showed that theology had never been an isolated discipline, but that on the contrary it had constantly sought to integrate into its researches the latest scientific developments, whether in history, linguistics, psychology or whatever.

These remarks were accompanied by a special commendation for the Pontifical Biblical Institute (usually known as the Biblicum) which was celebrating the sixtieth anniversary of its foundation. It was set up by Pope Saint Pius X in 1909, at the height of the Modernist crisis. John Paul did not recall this aspect of its history, but he had dug out the founding apostolic letter, *Vinea Electa*, which declared that the purpose of the new Institute would be 'that biblical studies and related studies would be more effectively pursued in the sense of the Catholic

Church' (7 May 1909). It is a matter of history that the professors of the Biblicum have had their moments of embarrassment and their moments of glory. For during the Modernist period they helped to formulate the highly conservative decrees of the Pontifical Biblical Commission between 1909 and 1915: they were effectively repealed in 1955 with the declaration of Freedom with Regard to the Early Decrees of the Pontifical Biblical Commission. The Biblicum's moment of glory came during Vatican II when its professors were frequently attacked by right-wing bishops, who suspected them, rightly, of providing the 'progressives' with scriptural ammunition. John Paul confined himself to recalling why it was founded.

Gregorian professors, finally, were urged to be 'creative' and the students were exhorted to learn from each other in this international community, for, he told them, 'the sense of catholicity and universal openness is the life-blood of the Church'. There was an oblique reference to Schillebeeckx in the final apostrophe on the theme 'Christmas is coming': 'In a few days' time, we will be reliving the ineffable mystery of the birth in time of God's eternal Word. God comes forward to meet those who seek him. He has the features, the voice and the gestures of a human being. In Christ the invisible becomes God-with-us, Emmanuel.' It was a fine expression of high Chalcedonian christology. It was repeated again and again in the sermons throughout the Christmas season.

The evening at the Gregorian was not quite over. On a table to the left of John Paul II was a pile of books, the combined output of the Gregorian professors over the past two years. It groaned under the weight of heavy tomes. Among them was Jean Galot's *Cristo Contestato*. Later that evening, after supper, Galot was presented to the Pope. 'I think we've met before', said John Paul. 'Of course you have,' a bystander remarked *sotto voce*, 'he's your Grand Inquisitor.' For the truth was that some of the Gregorian professors were ashamed at the behaviour of their colleague, Galot, and thought that he had not observed the 'decencies' of theological discussion. Others thought that he was simply wrong about Schillebeeckx.

But it was difficult to put that to the Pope on what was, after all, meant to be a festive occasion. That illustrated a more general problem: how could theologians get through to John Paul II and put it to him that there were alternative approaches to theology about which Galot was ignorant? What nobody present – except John Paul – knew at the time was that Küng had already been condemned. He kept this knowledge to himself.

A narrative like this does not have to 'conclude'. It stops, at a convenient point in time. Evaluation is a more subjective matter. But it seems reasonable to conclude that John Paul II has tried so far in his pontificate to extend a 'Polish view' of theology to the universal Church. Other Churches have different experiences of open discussion, of agreeing to differ without charges of disloyalty. Already other theologians are on the list of the CDF. Files have been opened on Charles E. Curran of the Catholic University of Washington; Leonardo Boff, a Brazilian 'theologian of liberation'; and John J. McNeill, an American Jesuit who has written a sympathetic book on homosexuality. And there will be others. For if the premise of the pontificate is that theologians have got out of hand, then it follows logically that they should be brought back to order and sound discipline. But there is always a price to be paid for repressive actions in the Church. They may check supposedly erroneous developments, they may reassure those who want to be told that 'nothing has changed or will change', they may bring comfort to the impenitent right wing (and there are well-founded rumours of a reconciliation with Archbishop Marcel Lefebvre), but they also alienate Christians within and without the Church. The Church is always in a state of tension between its 'ideal image' and its actual life. Ideally it is the home of truth-seeking, love, light, mutual encouragement, growth in the Spirit, prayer, harmony, reconciled diversity. In practice it can become, for a time, a place of fear, anxiety, denunciations, neurosis. When that happens, the well-meaning defence of orthodoxy becomes a counter-witness to the Gospel.

Fortunately no historical parallels are entirely apt, but

the pontificate of John Paul II (who perhaps should have taken the name of Pius XIII) begins to resemble in some respects the pontificate of Pope Saint Pius X. (Incidentally, the *advocatus diaboli* was not allowed to bring in his treatment of the Modernists.) Then as now the Pope is popular. Then as now theological work was discouraged except within the safest of limits. Then as now denunciation – for a process must start from someone – is part of the system. Then as now bureaucratic and institutional answers are given to theological and scientific problems. Then as now theologians were made to wonder: who will be next?

But there are four major differences between the early years of the century and its last twenty years. First, the basic lesson of the Modernist crisis has been learned. There is no theologian alive today who wishes to reduce dogmatic formulations merely to 'the expression of religious feeling'. The 'subjectivism' of the Modernists – if indeed there was a coherent movement worthy of the name, a fact that is disputed by some scholars – holds no power to charm. It was rightly reproved by the *magisterium*, however unworthy, disreputable, squalid and unjust its methods.

Secondly, contemporary Catholic theology can base itself squarely on the teaching of Vatican II, whereas the unfortunate Modernists could find no such support in the immediate Catholic tradition. This does not mean that Vatican II said the last word or can provide answers to questions it never asked. But it did represent an irrevocable commitment to certain positions, notably on ecumenism, the Church's self-understanding and its need to learn from the world. It can be re-edited, but not revoked.

Thirdly, the Church and the world have moved on since the early years of the century. Theology is no longer an internal ecclesiastical affair for specialists. It begins to involve the whole people of God. One does not need to be a professional theologian to feel injustice. In the Modernist crisis society was still in the paternalistic phase in which public opinion could be disregarded with impunity. But now ordinary people have been told so often in homilies that 'You are the Church' that they have ended up by believing it.

Finally, there is the hope that John Paul II will be unhappy in the role of unyielding autocrat which Saint Pius X so readily embraced. Having made his point, he could now relax. He has a philosophy which stresses the role of listening and learning, of being perpetually open to new experiences. It is not too late to hope that he may put it into practice. The enthusiastic applause of vast crowds is no substitute for the free consent of the intellectually committed.

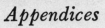

Appendices

Appendix 1. *Schillebeeckx's Written 'Clarification'*

Answer of Edward Schillebeeckx O.P., dated 13 April 1977, to the Questionnaire No. 46/66 addressed to him by the Congregation for the Doctrine of Faith

> Note: The questionnaire is here referred to as the Dossier and 'the book' means *Jesus – An Experiment in Christology*.

A preliminary answer which will determine all the other answers must be given, because I have the clear impression that most of the questions depend upon certain presuppositions.

As I said repeatedly in my book, it is to be thought of as a prologomenon, and demands other books for its completion. My second book on Jesus will appear within a few weeks. My plan was to provide a trilogy:

1) In volume one (the book under consideration) I wanted to find out what a rigorous historical method could yield up about Jesus' appearance on the stage of our history, and then to follow the itinerary (*itinerarium mentis*) of the disciples who met a Jew called Jesus, and after his death came to profess solemnly that he was risen and that he was in reality the Son of God, the second person of the Blessed Trinity.

2) In the second volume which is about to appear, I try to set down a New Testament christology, that is, I ask how the Pauline Epistles, the Gospel of John, the Pastoral and Catholic Epistles, Hebrews, and the Book of Revelation saw Christ. This is a matter of the direct exegesis of texts from the New Testament canon; it is no longer, as in volume one, a matter of the scientific reconstruction of Christian traditions that pre-dated the New Testament.

3) In a third volume (which I have only just begun) I intend to provide a systematic treatment of the doctrines

of the Church and of the Spirit (ecclesiology and pneumatology) that were already implied in the first two volumes.

A first conclusion is that one should not try to discover in the first volume material that will be explicitly dealt with in the second volume, still less the synthesis of the third volume. That is why I call the first volume, which is being challenged, a first 'sounding'. However, I have already concluded the first three parts of volume one with a first, provisional and rather short synthesis, because without it I was afraid that some readers would perhaps have been disconcerted by a purely historical approach which would have been complemented by a reflection in faith only in the second volume.

All this is the background to my first volume. Furthermore, about a year before my book appeared, there had been published a well-known anti-Christian book by the German Augstein. This came after a series of pamphlets which were allegedly on 'the real Jesus'. Thousands of Christians read this book and others like it, and were shattered: they had the feeling that the Church had been telling them fables and legends and that now at last historical science had unmasked this duplicity. Augstein was believed to have demonstrated that the Christ of history could not support the weight that the Church was supposed to have built up around the historical phenomenon of Jesus. What is more, all the newspapers had articles on Augstein's book, which also prompted many other little books on the so-called 'true' Jesus.

An answer was needed, not so much to refute Augstein, but to say something to those Christians who were confused about christology, not by theologians but by books such as these. That is what, to the best of my ability, I tried to do. (That is also the reason why the cover of the Dutch edition of the book was *black* – as an answer to the black cover of Augstein's book.)

Thus my project was primarily pastoral or, if you prefer it (though I don't like the term), apologetic. That is why I followed the same strictly historical method, in its most radical form, in order to attain to the actions and words of Jesus which could act as *signs* for all men of good will, signs which might enable them to understand the faith-response of the disciples of the historical phenomenon that is Jesus. So in this first volume I wanted to show that the apostolic faith is not an arbitrary superstructure, but that it is brought into existence by the person, the message, the works and the death of Jesus himself. Not that I was trying to *prove* faith by historical analysis: that would be absurd, as I point out three times in the course of the book (pp. 33, 103, 259). But I was trying to show that there were enough historical data, resistant to all historical criticism, to permit us to *understand* that and how the apostolic faith is itself the flowering (I usually speak of the 'reflection of', so the 'fruit') on the level of faith of Jesus who was living in Palestine. It is obvious that it is faith alone that can see in the acts and words of Jesus the divine action of the sovereign God; but that at least implies that it ought to be possible to indicate what these acts and words are which led the early Church to the awesome statement of faith that this man is God become man.

When one embarks on such a project, one must be honest with history, in the sense that one can only affirm as historically certain what is so according to the most rigorous demands of historical method. Anything one can arrive at in this way is (as I say frequently in my book) a great gain. But on the other hand, to bring into the analysis at this point data from faith or divine intervention or Church dogmas would spoil the whole enterprise, because that would already imply an act of faith. The Catholic exegete R. Schnackenburg has frequently said that the time had come to gather together all that is historically certain, in the strict historical sense, about Jesus. So the objection raised by the Dossier – that I show a preference for radical Protestant exegesis – is a total misunderstanding of the intention of this first volume. It presupposes that I should have done in the first volume what I proposed to do in the second volume. To establish a minimum of historical data was the best that could be hoped for in this project; or at any rate, it was better than trying to pass off as historical matters that could not be historically verified. Even this 'minimum' (and there's quite a lot of it!) is enough to raise in non-prejudiced minds a *religious question* which, obviously, can only be answered by an act of faith or of non-faith: who is Jesus?

That is why I do not say anywhere in my book that the *historical* image of Jesus, i.e. what historical science can recover of his image, is the norm and criterion of our faith, as the Dossier asserts (pp. 5f). That is clean contrary to what I say. Furthermore, it would be the most monstrous absurdity that a theologian, whether Catholic or Protestant, could perpetrate. Yet in my book I went to great trouble to make a clear distinction between 'the Jesus of history' (as he lived in the land of Palestine) and 'the historical Jesus' (i.e. the abstract picture of him that historical science can reach). It is 'the Jesus of history', living in Palestine, who is for me the norm and the criterion of faith. It is he who is the source and the cause of apostolic faith, whose concrete content is as it were 'filled out' by 'the Jesus of history' – and not by any abstract result derived from scientific history. At the same time, it is by means of a historical reconstruction that one can recover what it was in Jesus that led his disciples and contemporaries to their apostolic faith. If it had been my intention to provide an exegesis of the New Testament in this first volume (as I indeed do in the second volume, using different methods to those employed in the first volume), the objection that I have a preference for the most radical exegetes would be serious and well-founded. But the contrary is true for anyone who has grasped the purpose of my first volume (as is explained pp. 17–40).

What is more I even say that the Jesus of history (living in Palestine) is not the norm and criterion 'in the abstract', because we do not know of him except through the gospels, witnesses of our faith. Thus the starting point for our faith is *neither* Jesus as such *nor* the early Church as such, but *both together*. That is to say that it is Jesus, but coming down to us through the witness of the first

Christians (the Church); or it is the first Christians (the Church) but in so far as their witness corresponds to and is objectively 'fulfilled' by what Jesus was and said and by his person. The entire first part of my book together with its long introduction is an attempt to explain the unbreakable unity between the objective historical appearance that is Jesus and his Church. I add that this unified whole (Jesus and the New Testament witness to him) is based on the Jesus of history and not the historical Jesus (i.e. the result of scientific historical research); and that this unified whole has total priority over the apostolic faith which merely reflects for us what Jesus truly was (book pp. 21, 50, 46, 57, 481, etc.).

I repeated all this at length in an article which was a reply to the Protestant Professor H. Berkhof, 'Fides quaerens intellectum historicum' (in Nederlands Theologisch Tijdschrift, 1975, vol. 29, No. 4, pp. 332–49). Furthermore I say quite explicitly that the historical research in my book is conducted not in the manner of some neutral or radical historian but 'in a spirit of faith'. However, such an enterprise demands that the data of faith cannot enter into the process of the historical research itself, because in that case all the apologetic advantages of such an enterprise would be frittered away; it would be paralysed and negated from the outset. I have to admit that this way of approach to Christianity is rather unusual at the present time. That is why I warned my readers in the Foreword by telling them that my approach to christology is 'unconventional', while adding that my intention is to present a *Christian* christology.

This method further demands that 'the starting point' (which is not the starting point of a christological synthesis, as the Dossier suggests, but the starting point of scientific and historical research – which is quite a different matter) should be the encounter of some Jews with another Jew called Jesus, so with a human being, a man, that is, a human person. A historian does not begin from the fact that the Jews met God in this fellow Jew. It was the meeting with this Jew that was the *primary* experience of the disciples. But I immediately add (something forgotten by the Dossier) that at the end of this itinerary of the disciples with Jesus it should become clear whether their first impression was right or wrong, and above all the real *identity* of this man should be clarified (book, p. 33). The whole work was conceived and written to show how provisional their first impression was, because in the end one cannot simply say that Jesus is a human person *tout court* (p. 667).

The Dossier, however, has taken this 'starting point' as an ontological statement, and consequently it has great difficulty in understanding how I can harmonize my first statement with my second – which is a faulty way of setting up the problem. For there is nothing to harmonize! There is not one ontological statement which has to be harmonized with another, but two phases or stages in the journey or itinerary of the apostles: (1) their first encounter and their first impression, and (2) their final assessment after the death of Jesus, and this is an act of faith, identifying Jesus ultimately and ontologically as the Son of God. Of the 133 international reviews of my book, all but four or five understood that this was my intention. It was precisely this new angle on Jesus that seemed so helpful to almost all my readers. The exceptions were those who insisted on giving an ontological reading to the book, and as a result misunderstood it completely. With one exception (which I will mention later) all the questions in the Dossier presuppose this ontological reading, whereas the book should be read as a reconstruction of the itinerary made by the apostles, who in their encounter with the man Jesus conclude in the end by an ontological statement of faith: this man was and is truly the Son of God. He was this before this encounter, even at his conception, even as pre-existent; but that is the ultimate act of faith, not the start of the journey. And my purpose was to provide a historical 'initiation' (*manducatio*) for worried Christians: it was to trace the genesis of apostolic faith.

The dogma of Chalcedon was the undisputed presupposition for me in the work of '*fides quaerens intellectum historicum*' (faith seeking historical understanding);

134

without this, I would not have embarked upon this long and arduous quest. Yet the Dossier throughout calls into question my faith in this Council. Why? I simply do not understand. What is more, I say quite explicitly in my book: as for me 'I have no trouble at all with any of this [the Council of Chalcedon] ... it [the dogma] is straight gospel' (book, pp. 564–7). The Dossier nowhere quotes this crucial text. But I must also add that many Christians have problems in understanding the philosophical background to notions such as 'hypostasis, nature and person' which later underwent considerable semantic changes. In the ordinary course of things faith does not determine semantic changes (though it did in the era of the great christological struggles in the fourth and fifth centuries, but not after that). It is a matter of fact that words like 'nature' and 'person', even for cultivated people today, no longer have the same meaning that they had at the time of Chalcedon, even though experts can demonstrate by the most elaborate exegesis that these ideas have not essentially been changed. But that is not the level which concerns ordinary believers.

The purpose of the fourth part of my book was precisely to translate the dogma of Chalcedon into the language of the faithful today. Even the Dossier has to admit that I 'tend towards' the dogma of Chalcedon, while forgetting that it is this dogma itself that impelled me to find a form of expression which would be intelligible for Christians without having first to convert them – in order to remain faithful to it – to a philosophy or to semantic usages which are foreign and incomprehensible. The authors of the Dossier brought pre-conceptions of a different kind to their reading of my book, and they also assume that I share in an anti-Chalcedonian attitude (that I, too, detect in the literature and against which I react strongly!). A theologian should be read for what he has to say (*prout jacet*) and not in the light of a theological tendency that he rejects.

ANSWERS IN DETAIL

Section I HISTORICAL METHOD

1) *Preference for the most radical exegetical tendencies*

I deny categorically that I have a preference for *exegesis* 'according to the radical wing of Protestant scholars' (and volume two will provide a complete refutation of this suggestion). But in volume one I had to follow the most relentless historico-critical method in order to have a secure historical basis. Otherwise my book would have made no sense. So I do not provide in volume one an *exegesis* of New Testament texts at all (that is the subject of volume two); instead, through the mediation of these texts I try to reach the pre-New Testament traditions.

2) *Exegetical reduction*

Historical science as such is reductive by its very method; that is why as such it is incapable of bringing faith. But it is nevertheless able to reconstruct the historical basis in which the pre-New Testament Christians detected and believed in the salvific action of God. This scientific reconstruction enables us to understand that apostolic faith is not a superstructure but an answer in faith to the phenomenon of history called Jesus. So this historical reduction has nothing whatever to do, directly or indirectly, with a theological reduction (which it could be for an unbeliever, but never for me for whom 'faith seeks historical understanding'). But on the other hand to pre-judge the historical data by a non-historical method (e.g. by faith) would wreck the entire pastoral project of an 'initiation' (*manducatio*) into faith.

3) *Premature Hermeneutics*

The objection would hold only if I had provided a hermeneutical exegesis of New Testament faith (something that I do in the second volume). The scope of volume one was the underlying traditions and therefore the origins of early Christianity, and nothing more.
(a) Nowhere in my book do I say that I see Christ solely

in functional terms – as the Dossier alleges. Faithful to my project'I say that it is only through what Jesus said and underwent (his death), that is through his 'functions', that the way to his person and identity is opened up – at least to the eye of faith. Along with W. Schlier, for example, I reject the choice between a 'substantial' and a 'functional' theology. This is anyway a modern distinction, unknown in late antiquity.

(b) The Dossier overlooks the fact that for me the eschatological prophet is *messianic*. This title is not in my view 'minimalist' (as the Dossier wrongly assumes) but on the contrary is one of the most maximalist of all the pre-New Testament titles because it indicates the universal importance, value and relevance of Jesus for all human history (as I explain more fully and with more evidence in my second volume). Thus the second basic response of the disciples of Jesus is based upon their initial profession that he was the eschatological and *messianic* prophet, an infinitely greater new Moses. When I say in a precise context that Christ is the non-messiah, this clearly means that he denied the royal, military and nationalistic messianism found in certain contemporary Jewish milieux. But there was another form of royal messianism which identified the Messiah with the eschatological prophet (as has now been proved in a dozen studies of the Johannine tradition, as I show in volume two).

What is more, I was looking for the very *first* expression of Christian faith, already pregnant with its final expression. And I warn my readers that this first expression or 'an experience of recognizing-and-recollecting (*erkenning* and *herkenning*), as first articulated, is not *ipso facto* the richest or most subtle one' (book, p. 54). Furthermore to trace the history of the evolution of dogma after the death of Jesus through to the last book of the New Testament is already an important part of the 'understanding of faith' (and it must of course be continued after the end of the New Testament as well). What I tried to do, therefore, was not a premature interpretation (hermeneutic), but an interpretation of a very early stage in the development of a faith that was becoming the apostolic faith of the New Testament.

I am also blamed for identifying 'God's cause' with 'man's cause' (which is in fact a tendency in some of the literature but not in my book). The Dossier omits to mention that for me the contrary is the case and has the priority, and that 'man's cause' is 'God's cause', i.e. that God himself is man's salvation and that God wills the salvation of man (as I explain at some length in my second volume). Views are attributed to me that I have nowhere put forward.

4) *Jesus of Nazareth, norm and criterion of every interpretation*

The heading is excellent. But this 'Jesus of Nazareth' is the Jesus of history and not the 'historical Jesus' – the reconstruction that results from historical research (book, pp. 67–70), an essential and crucial distinction. I say that the Jesus of history, living in Palestine, is the origin and cause, the norm and the criterion, and the objective determinant of apostolic faith. I simply add that for that very reason an honest historical reconstruction *can help us to understand* how the apostolic faith was in fact determined by the objective historical existence of Jesus. That is the whole point of my book, as I explained afterwards at some length in an article in *Kulturleven* (1975, vol. 42, pp. 81–93) in which I introduced it. So I deny that one can find in my book the assertion that would be very odd for a Christian: 'In the end the norm and criterion of this interpretation of Jesus is the Jesus of our historical knowledge' (Dossier, p. 6. I do not understand how the Dossier can say that after having read pp. 52–7 of my book. Cf. also pp. 44f.).

5) *The 'offer' of Jesus and 'interpretative answers' to it*

For me as for the Dossier this is a highly important question. But I am afraid that the same words are used, in different senses, on each side. I use this terminology to say what Saint Thomas Aquinas said, namely that objective revelation becomes a formal revelation in the *auditus fidei* ('faith's listening') and the *assensus fidei* ('the assent of faith'). A revelation that was not heard would remain an unknown X. For me the 'offer' is simply another word for what is 'objectively revealed' in Christ. That is why I do not speak of 'offer' (*aanbod*) *tout court* but always of *werkelijkheidsaanbod,* i.e. the objective reality which is given to man in Jesus. This offer is made up of what Jesus says and does and suffers (and so also of his death) and in the end of his person (whose identity the book seeks by following the journey of the apostles).

The basic epistemology of Saint Thomas (*'ad modum recipientis recipitur'*) means that the articulating response of faith will always take the form of an *interpretation* (as I explain in my book, pp. 48f, 54f). But I get the feeling that the Dossier confuses my terminology of 'interpretative faith' (which means the 'articulation of faith' according to the medieval term, *articulus fidei*) with the learned term coined by W. Marxsen (see in the appendix of Technical Information 'Interpretament', p. 746) which I explicitly reject (for further details cf. the article already mentioned in *Nederlands Theologisch Tijdschrift,* 1975, vol. 29, esp. pp. 333f).

Thus, when I say that the response of faith is always interpretative, I mean by that that revelation or the Word of God comes to us in the mould of human language – and in this case, of a language borrowed from the Jewish religious tradition. But I add an important precision: the content of the Jewish key-words (Son of Man, Son of God, Messiah, the Holy One of God, eschatological prophet, etc.) was 'transformed, regauged and corrected by the force of Jesus' own authority and historic impact' (book, pp. 28f), that is, by the reality that is the Christ. Therefore (as I show in over fifty pages of volume two) the term 'interpretation' in no way signifies some further *arbitrary* and *subjective* determination, but is rather the expression of the revealed content in a historical framework.

Here is an example of another misunderstanding. The Dossier quotes pp. 576–9 where I make use of a rather complicated distinction borrowed from modern cultural anthropology. A distinction is made between three kinds of historical change: (a) rapid and ephemeral changes, (b) long term changes (called *Epochale Denkmodellen* by B. Welte and K. Rahner) and (c) changes which require millennia and are therefore imperceptible. The fundamental mistake of the Dossier (and it explains a lot) is to bring together these anthropological distinctions with another distinction which I make in a quite different context, namely a *linguistic* distinction (without ontological value) between 'first-order statements' and 'second-order statements'. This has nothing whatever to do with the triple distinction which concerns historical change.

The linguistic distinction, as is well known, has nothing to do with the idea of change or evolution (primary or secondary) but is concerned with the structure of our discourse or spoken language. When a statement refers directly to a reality, it is called in linguistics a first-order statement; when on the other hand it refers to another previous statement, it is said to be 'second-order'. Thus 'second-order' does not imply being derived or of 'secondary importance', as the Dossier appears to think. A second-order statement can, ontologically speaking, have more value and richness than a first-order statement. Consequently the historical assertion (yet another level), for example that the first Christians considered Jesus above all as the eschatological prophet (which is purely a matter of historical research), while these same Christians (or the next generation) later say that Jesus is the Son of God made man, is an instance of the distinction. But one cannot conclude from that that the first statement is more important or that the second does not contain a richer reality as a development of what was implicit in the first statement. The Dossier accuses me of saying the contrary of what my book plainly says (cf. p. 549). All that can be said is that second-order statements are more 'reflexive' (which is why I say – but now we enter the psychological order – that someone who really believes in Jesus as his definitive and eschatological salvation and that this salvation comes from God, already believes in all the christological dogmas which all try to work out the implications of this first-order statement).

It follows that I cannot understand what the Dossier says on p. 8 ('Thus light is thrown ...'). These remarks have nothing to do with my book. The conclusions are false, because the premises are neither mine nor those of my book. For me first-order statements are pregnant with all the later explanations. The Dossier systematically takes every remark that such and such a statement 'came later' as meaning 'therefore superfluous' or 'of less value' or – much more seriously – 'therefore mutable'. I really do not know what there is in my book that gives rise to such misinterpretations. Perhaps one of the reasons for this faulty interpretation is my use of the expression *overschildering door de kerk* which literally means repainting or touching-up an original painting. Obviously this is a metaphor or an image which tries to make vivid what can be expressed more cumbersomely: the re-presentation or the faithful interpretation of what Jesus said in different circumstances. In scholastic language one could call it an 'application' of what Jesus said in new circumstances.

But the Dossier finds in this a certain relativism, an 'addition' attributed to the Church without any objective foundation in Jesus himself – something which falsifies my book. Once again, the Dossier fails to understand that it was my intention to take my readers through all the stages of the disciples, step by step, until the final flowering of the profession of the divinity of Christ. It is precisely the courage to follow this way – however difficult and arduous but in the end rewarding – that led several readers to say on finishing my book, 'Yes, it is true.' They had followed the same road to Emmaus to the point at which they could (for some of them once again) say: 'It is true, I confess that Jesus is the Christ, the Son of God.' This is exactly the opposite to what one finds in much contemporary literature (most of it untheological) which reduces Jesus to some kind of prophet who merely proclaimed a humanist and social transformation of society. My book is entirely directed against such a tendency!

Obviously historians are free to say (provided they can produce historical arguments) that here or there I made historical mistakes, or that this or that is less historically certain than I say. I would be the first to agree and in the Foreword to my book I invite them to make their criticisms. I have already received criticism on detailed points and accept it. But more than forty specialists, historians and exegetes have written to me or said in their reviews that the fundamental and overall thesis of my book is difficult to falsify. Furthermore, a dozen or so articles on the Johannine and pre-Johannine tradition have provided confirmation for my views on the eschatological and messianic prophet.

While on the point of the triple distinction that I made, I should mention the statement of the Dossier (referring to p. 581 *et seq* of my book): 'Trinity, redemption, grace ... none of these seem any longer to be self-evident'. That is said not in the context of the linguistic distinction, but in that of the triple cultural distinction. I was thinking of the *Epochale Denkmodellen*. These dogmas are talked about with the aid of other 'thinking models' and thus to the uninitiated person *seem* to be different. But when one becomes aware of the new 'model' one realizes that one is dealing with the same reality (which does not imply that every model is equally satisfactory). That is what my book says when it is read straightforwardly. That is why I wrote pages 576-9. And it is such distinctions that reassure rather than disconcert the faithful and permit them once again to believe in Jesus Christ as true God and true man (apart, I have to admit, from some followers of Archbishop Marcel Lefebvre).

SECTION II
1) *'A starting point: Jesus as human person'*
I have already explained that this is the starting point not for a christology but for historical research, which

142

can never encounter a God made man. All the ontological efforts made in the Dossier to harmonize the statements made in Part I with those made in Part IV of my book are *extra campum*, off the point. There is no need to harmonize anything. What one has to do is to follow the road from the start (first impressions, vague and imprecise) right to the end (final impression, expressed as a confession of faith). It is only at the end that Jesus' identity is fully revealed. And it is here that the ontological problem begins: how can a man be the true Son of God? In my book I trace the *process* which leads to the full flowering of faith. The Dossier can only see everywhere ontological and metaphysical assertions.

In the fourth part of my book, in the provisional synthesis, one reaches ontological statements about the person of Jesus. But at this level I never speak of the human person of Jesus, but of Jesus who is 'personally human'. At this point the Dossier adds '*sic!*' So it has noticed the unusual nature of this expression without wondering why I used it. (In any case, the Dossier's translation is incorrect. It translates: 'Cet homme ... dans les limites d'une manière d'être personnelle-humaine.' It should read: '... une manière d'être personnellement humaine'.) I say that his way of being human is personalist and nothing more. Only once do I use the expression 'human person' in the ontological context but then it is precisely *to deny* that the Christ can be called a human person (book, p. 667). In this way I wanted to safeguard the understanding of Chalcedon and at the same time a contemporary understanding.

For most modern readers a 'human person' is something quite different semantically from what we find in conciliar and scholastic vocabulary. Must they first of all be converted to a specific philosophical view before they can be led to the apostolic faith? Surely the answer must be no. Now a concrete man with an *anima spiritualis*, endowed with human will, intelligence and love, is for most of our readers a 'human person'. But I don't use this expression and prefer to say always that Jesus is 'personally human', which is a quite different thing. It is the only way to save the terminology of Chalcedon: the humanity of Jesus is personalist, formally spiritual. Even a neo-Chalcedonian can accept that much. Chalcedon itself does not speak of an an-hypostasis (cf. glossary, p. 745), a neo-Chalcedonian term as Mgr Lebon and Mgr Charles Moeller have shown, but of *unus et idem* (one and the same) who is true God and true man. That is what I maintain throughout my book.

But I also take into account the kind of usage with which my readers are familiar. For them a concrete human nature, formally spiritual, is a human person. I find this usage incorrect, and that is why I never speak of 'human person' but of the 'personally human' to show that the concrete reality of Jesus is personalist, formally spiritual, and that there is nothing lacking in his humanity. (This is something to which our readers are very sensitive: they do not want there to be anything humanly lacking in Christ.) Most of my reviewers have understood what I was doing, and some of them – alas – even regretted that my christology remained traditional, conservative and Chalcedonian!

What has just been said also provides the answer to the question about en-hypostasis and an-hypostasis. I simply deny that there was anything lacking in the humanity of Jesus (just as St Thomas denies it). But I also know by experience that the idea that 'another' person can personalize a 'human nature' is incomprehensible for most of our readers. How then can one make sense of the dogma? I did this by means of the notion of *hypostatic identification*, i.e. not a union of two persons, human and divine, but an (of course ontological) identification of the second person of the Trinity with a formally spiritual human nature. In my opinion that is the traditional hypostatic union in its pure form. And explained in this way, all my readers have understood and accepted it.

I have given this explanation in more than twenty lectures in Germany, Belgium and Holland, and so reached about 10,000 people who had already studied my book (or most of them had); and this explanation satisfied them fully, whereas when I used to say that the divine person acts as the person of a human nature, they were completely baffled. When one says that a divine person is identified with full humanity (body and soul), they can understand. Now I say: that is precisely the dogma of Chalcedon. So the suspicion in the Dossier, that I support the 'anti-Chalcedonian project of a host of contemporary theologians', would be rightly rejected by almost all my non-prejudiced readers.

2) *'Jesus – not as Messiah, but as eschatological prophet'*
This opposition between 'not' and 'but' is found nowhere in my book and goes against its fundamental intention. In my book the eschatological prophet is not the precursor of the Messiah (as in certain Jewish currents) but the Messiah himself. He is the eschatological and Messianic prophet (cf. e.g. p. 477). In the second volume I provide more evidence to show that the eschatological prophet is royal, priestly and messianic: the mosaic messiah.

What is more, I do not posit a time gap (as the Dossier does) between what *Jesus* thought and what the *disciples* made of it. The whole thrust of my book is to show that what the disciples say of Jesus after the death of the Lord is the reflection, the articulate and fully conscious explicitation of what Jesus really was and said. I resolutely deny that the Dossier's phrase about 'the absence of any messianic project in Jesus' applies to my book.

3) *Jesus, servant of Yahweh, handed over for our sins*
For me this assertion is the high point of what I was trying to say in the book. But the Dossier presents it as though it were an objection.

Where in my book do I deny that 'the words of institution of the Eucharist' are not anchored in the history of Jesus? The Dossier says that I have adopted the views of W. Marxsen! But in this connection the only reference is to the Catholic exegete H. Schürmann (cf. Notes, p. 699). With him I distinguish between two textual levels in the New Testament: (a) already formulated liturgical texts (which therefore presuppose the liturgical life of the early Church), and (b) an older level of which I say with F. Hahn that it belongs to 'the primeval rock of the tradition' (book, p. 376f). The Dossier insinuates that *therefore* I deny the institution of the Eucharist by Christ. They seem not to have read my book but that of W. Marxsen. I say explicitly that these eucharistic texts faithfully articulate the historical words and actions of Jesus (pp. 376f).

I admit that I say nothing, at least directly, about a sacrificial soteriology: that is almost true. True: because it is the theme of volume two (as I explain twice in volume one, pp. 35 and 669). *Almost* true (and therefore not true) because, as a prelude to volume two, I say explicitly that in the end the death of Jesus was taken up in his plan of salvation (pp. 310f, 542f). The implications of that statement are fully developed in volume two, including concepts such as sacrifice, satisfaction and so on.

4) *Jesus and God, his Father*

Frankly, I found this part of the Dossier particularly painful. In reaction against a humanizing tendency which tends to strike out Jesus' constitutive relationship with his Father, the pages on God as the *Abba* of Jesus Christ are the very heart of my book. For reasons which I do not understand, the Dossier links them up with certain Protestant theses from the nineteenth century. It is precisely through this conscious and unique relationship of Jesus with his Father that I find a way of approach that enables me to affirm the hypostatic union (cf. also the article in *Nederlands Theologisch Tijdschrift*, 1975, vol. 29, p. 345f). The Dossier minimizes everything I say in this chapter, and takes as the basis of its case the fact that I say that the word as such (*Abba*) is not decisive. (Once again, the requirements of a rigorous historical study have been forgotten.) In my view it is not this word as such which accounts for the unique relation of Jesus to his Father (*even though* the use of the term was totally unknown in contemporary Judaism); the decisive point is the almost exclusive use of the term in the context of the person, the preaching and the life of Jesus. The Dossier in fact states my own position – but as an objection. But then the Dossier seems to hesitate about its interpretation of my book in the paragraph beginning, 'Are you not afraid that ...'

I agree that there is room for discussion of the sentence: 'Jesus never posited himself (beside the rule of God) as the *second* subject of his proclamation' (p. 258 – though I think that it is historically justified). But I deny the conclusion drawn by the Dossier. For the gospels (and for me too) the Kingdom of God is Jesus. I merely deny that that statement is made from the outset (and I was trying to retrace the itinerary and the successive statements of the disciples). I have often insisted that in the Q tradition, to take up an attitude for or against the Kingdom of God is to take up an attitude for or against Jesus (adding that it is highly likely that these words are authentic words of Jesus). On the lips of Jesus himself there is an implicit identification between the Kingdom and Jesus. The explicit identification (especially in the Johannine tradition) is therefore only a legitimate working out of the awareness that Jesus had of himself, and that is what my book is designed to show! But the Dossier seems to forget that the book was trying to follow the development of the pre-New Testament dogma.

5) *Easter as the turning point*

I am very grateful that the Dossier agrees that I profess 'the personal and bodily resurrection' of Jesus (two reviewers thought that I was denying it).

The Dossier, however, has difficulties with my explanation of the appearances. I have to concede that this is – I do not say the weakest part of my book, but – the part that is scientifically the most hypothetical. Before commenting on the question, I would like to refer to one of the most competent of my reviewers, Mgr Albert Descamps of Louvain (to whom Mgr Prignon could be added). Mgr Descamps has exegetical objections to my interpretation, although he adds quite explicitly that whatever one may think of it, it remains within Catholic orthodoxy. So it is a historical question only, provided at least one recognizes (as I do) that there is a divine revelation of Christ's resurrection. I accept what is *the point* intended in the resurrection narratives: the event is a pure grace of God in and through Christ who lives after his death with the Father in such a way that the affirmation of the bodily resurrection of Jesus is not the result of 'flesh and blood' but of divine revelation. That is the heart of the dogma.

I also concede (in the popular book mentioned by the Dossier) that historically there is no need to deny visual elements in the paschal event. The centre point of my argument is merely to deny that such visual elements are the *foundation* of our faith in the resurrection (as is often heard in sermons, with the result that some of the faithful are offended and the dogma appears ridiculous). Furthermore, I was approaching the question from a historical point of view and looking for the given circumstances, accessible to a historian, in which this divine revelation was presented. I do not deny *a priori* than an apparition can mediate divine revelation. I simply say that there existed models of conversion, presented in the form of appearances, and that I detect this same model in the biblical appearance narratives. Obviously one can discuss whether my exegesis is plausible on this point. Here I await counter-arguments which would falsify my exegesis. So far they have not been forthcoming (though some reviewers have simply denied my position without giving any arguments).

But even when one disagrees with my interpretation, one should make an honest distinction between what I say and what I do not say. (a) I deny (once again against W. Marxsen) that faith in the resurrection is only a post-paschal *interpretation* of the pre-paschal life of Jesus (book, pp. 392–4). Because certain hasty readers had interpreted my book in this erroneous manner, in the third edition of the Dutch edition of the book I added five pages (pp. 528a–528e; not yet included in the English

148

translation) in which I make clear my rejection of R. Bultmann and W. Marxsen. (b) I do not neglect psychological (and therefore historical) realities, as the Dossier suggests. On the contrary I wanted to rid our preaching of a preoccupation with what happened historically in order to free it from the hocus-pocus with which it is commonly presented. I state that the intention of the narratives is to provide 'a specific and foundational witness' (as the Dossier rightly notes). I say quite clearly: 'One cannot deny that an intrinsic link is suggested in the New Testament between the resurrection of Jesus and the paschal experience, expressed through the model of the appearances' (p. 528a). Or again: 'From our analysis of the paschal experience, it is evident that one cannot separate the objective and the subjective aspect of the apostolic faith in the resurrection of Christ' (p. 528b), and that 'without confusing the two, the resurrection of Jesus – that is, what happened to Christ personally after his death – cannot be separated from the paschal experience of faith, work of the Holy Spirit' (p. 528b). (c) I also say – though in other words – that the paschal experience of the apostles is 'closed', over, *de facto* and *de jure* (as the Dossier has correctly perceived), while adding that Christians have to go through an analogous paschal experience of renewal of life based on the resurrection. (d) I insist that this 'conversion' of the apostles is not any kind of *metanoia* (which is the general law of all Christian life) but is the *'great turning point'* at which, after the death of Jesus and on the grounds of new grace events, 'the disciples recognize and confess him as the Christ' (p. 258b). There is therefore a true christophany: and that is the meaning of the appearances. Perhaps my use of the term 'conversion' in both the moral and christological sense leads to ambiguity. In any event, for me the christophany is essential in the vocabulary of conversion, just as the christophany is essential in the appearance stories: *ophthè*. It is the living Christ, the Risen One, who *opens their eyes* (the definitive element in these post-paschal experiences).

That 'where two or three are gathered in my name,

there am I in the midst of them' is perhaps 'the purest and most adequate expression of the paschal experience' (p. 528c) is quoted completely out of context in the Dossier (though I admit that my text is ambiguous). I quoted this biblical text to show the intrinsic link between the resurrection as something which happens to Christ and his glorified, heavenly presence in the Church. (That is the true context of the remark, which should not be taken as an expression of the structure of the paschal experience itself.) There is no presence of Christ to his Church without the resurrection (these pages were written against W. Marxsen).

SECTION III
1) *Incarnation and Trinity*
The Dossier congratulates me because in my book I 'come to the recognition of God as the trinitarian plenitude of the Father, the Son who appeared in Jesus, and the Spirit who animates the Church' (as though this affirmation were rather surprising for a Catholic theologian). But later on, the Dossier seems to suggest the contrary. I have already explained my position in Section II above. From this explanation it should be clear that all the abstract possibilities of interpretation, suggested by the Dossier, miss the point of my book. On rereading the whole context, I admit that my expression 'reciprocal en-hypostasis' could be equivocal, especially for those formed in the scholastic tradition. In fact I was using this terminology in an attempt to make comprehensible what the Greek Fathers call *perichoresis* and *theandrism*: the person of the Logos encloses the personalist humanity of Jesus and this concrete humanity does not remain outside of or extrinsic to the hypostasis of the Logos. The Dossier itself has to admit that in some places there seems to be a hint that 'we can hope for a renewed discovery of Chalcedon'! Chalcedon for me is the norm of all my theological research: I want to initiate Christians into this dogma, surfeited as they are with books which declare that 'God is dead' or that Jesus was no more than a man or a great prophet. If Chalcedon were

a dead letter for me, I would hardly have had the desire or the courage to write two books totalling more than 1400 pages.

2) *The Holy Trinity*
First, a point of detail. There is a misunderstanding about the quotation, 'God would be no God without creatures and Jesus of Nazareth' (p. 668). It is indeed an unusual expression, but it must be seen in context. For me as a disciple of St Thomas, any idea of (necessary) emanation is absurd. The creation and the incarnation are free acts of God. But God's freedom is not a *contingent 'liberum arbitrium'*. Contingency marks the effects of God, but not the divine act itself, which is the very essence of God himself, as Aquinas teaches. 'God would not be God without creation ...' would be completely false, if it were asserted *ex parte Dei* (from God's side), but it is not false if it is asserted *ex parte creaturarum* (from the creatures' side). In other words, *given* the contingent fact of the existence of creatures and of Jesus, God is essentially a Creator God and eternally the principle of the Incarnation, but in a divinely free act. This is the basis of God's immutability.

3) *Virginal Conception of Jesus*
On this point the Dossier has not misunderstood the meaning of my book, but it has forgotten that in it I say nothing either for or against this highly authentic tradition of the Church. In my first volume I studied the meaning of the virginal conception only as it appears in Matthew and Luke (and based my exegesis mainly on Catholic exegetes). In fact these exegetes have noted that there existed in the New Testament Church several tendencies on this question. One strand was unable to explain the divinity of Christ except by the virginal conception; there are other strands in the New Testament which do not posit this necessary link. Furthermore the exegetes note a tendency to dissociate the two concepts, in such a way that the stress is increasingly laid on the biological aspect of the virginal conception so that its

religious import is lost sight of (this happens especially in the Apocrypha).

In my book I did not deal with the virginal conception for its own sake, but only as an element in the pre-New Testament development of dogma: Jesus, recognized as the Christ in virtue of his resurrection; Jesus, recognized as the Christ already at his baptism; Jesus, recognized as the Christ from his birth; and Jesus recognized as the pre-existent Christ. The virginal conception as such is not studied in this context. One cannot therefore draw from it any conclusions about my personal position, which is not given in this first volume. Quite obviously, I agree that I will have to make my position clear in the second or third volume of my trilogy. For I admit that alongside sacred scripture there exists the great Christian tradition. But in volume one I leave the question open. As a theologian I could be reproached for leaving in the air certain important aspects of our faith. In my view that depends on the circumstances. Since my book was addressed principally to Catholics and other Christians who have difficulties with Christian dogma, I am convinced that Jesus' principle, 'You cannot bear them now' (John 16:12), has a legitimate pastoral application, *provided* that this silence does not concern the substantials of faith and furthermore is provisional.

4) *The Church*
I speak constantly about the Church in my book, but provisionally and prospectively. (The doctrine of the Church will be the subject of volume three, and in the three volumes there is a gradual upward movement towards the fulness of dogma, according to the pastoral and 'apologetic' intention of the trilogy.) In the first volume I speak of the Church in terms of 'Christian community' or 'the movement that gathered around Jesus'. Marginal Christians, or Christians on the edge of the Church (their number is growing, and they are not the worst), are not brought back to Christ by the ritual repetition of the word 'Church': on the contrary! I try to bring them there gently without alarming them by a

terminology which for them is already loaded with all the sins of Israel.

The Dossier offers an incorrect French translation of an interview I gave – and several times in Holland I have said in lectures how unhappy I was with it. The Dossier wrongly uses the phrase 'feeling of union', whereas I have always said that 'the feeling of union with Rome remains inviolable'. But I added that within this 'feeling of union', *affection* for Rome has been weakened or is even absent among theologians. That is a completely different matter! (And some Roman Congregations know what efforts certain theologians associated with the review *Concilium* have made to improve this situation.) Even if this intention was not faithfully conveyed in the interview, I find it extremely unlikely that the faithful were shocked by it.

Here, then, is my first attempt at an answer to the questionnaire. I think and I hope that a number of misunderstandings have been cleared up. Like the Dossier, I have spoken in complete frankness bearing in mind the good of the Church. With the Dossier I am convinced that there are in various churches christological tendencies which depart from the great Christian tradition. Along with the Dossier, I too wish to combat them. There seems to be a difference of method between the Dossier and my book in our efforts to challenge this infidelity. But the goal is the same, and that is the sole evangelical consolation that the Dossier brought me.

E. Schillebeeckx O.P.

Appendix 2. *Declaration of the Congregation for the Doctrine of Faith,* 15 December 1979

Declaration on Some Major Points in the Theological Doctrine of Professor Hans Küng.

The Church of Christ has received from God the mandate to keep and to safeguard the deposit of faith so that all the faithful, under the guidance of the Sacred *Magisterium* through which Christ himself exercises his role as teacher in the Church, may cling without fail to the faith once delivered to the saints, may penetrate it more deeply by accurate insights, and may apply it more thoroughly to life.[1]

In order to fulfil the important task entrusted to itself alone[2] the *Magisterium* of the Church avails itself of the work of theologians, especially those who in the Church have received from the authorities the task of teaching and who therefore have been designated in a certain way as teachers of the truth. In their research the theologians, like scholars in other fields, enjoy a legitimate scientific liberty, though within the limits of the method of sacred theology. Thus, while working in their own way, they seek to attain the same specific end as the *Magisterium* itself, namely, 'to preserve, to penetrate ever more deeply, to explain, to teach, to defend the sacred deposit of revelation; and in this way to illumine the life of the Church and of the human race with the light of divine truth'.[3]

It is necessary therefore that theological research and teaching should always be illumined with fidelity to the *Magisterium* since no one may rightly act as a theologian except in close union with the mission of teaching truth which is incumbent on the Church herself.[4] When such fidelity is absent, harm is done to all the faithful who, since they are bound to profess the faith which they have received from God through the Church, have a sacred right to receive the word of God uncontaminated, and so they expect that vigilant care should be exercised to keep the threat of error far from them.[5]

If it should happen, therefore, that a teacher of sacred doctrine chooses and disseminates as the norm of truth his own judgement and not the thought of the Church, and if he continues in his conviction, despite the use of all charitable means in his regard, then honesty itself demands that the Church should publicly call attention to his conduct and should state that he can no longer teach with the authority of the mission which he received from her.[6]

This canonical mission is in fact a testimony to a reciprocal trust: first, trust on the part of the competent authority that the theologian will conduct himself as a Catholic theologian in the work of his research and teaching; secondly, trust on the part of the theologian himself in the Church and in her integral teaching, since it is by her mandate that he carries out his task.

Since some of the writings – spread throughout many countries – and the teaching of Professor Hans Küng, a priest, are a cause of disturbance in the minds of the faithful, the Bishops of Germany and this Congregation for the Doctrine of Faith, acting in common accord, have several times counselled and warned him in order to persuade him to carry on his theological work in full communion with the authentic *Magisterium* of the Church.

In this spirit the Sacred Congregation for the Doctrine of Faith, in order to fulfil its role of promoting and safeguarding the doctrine of faith and morals in the universal Church,[7] issued a public document on 15 February 1975, declaring that some opinions of Professor Hans Küng were opposed in different degrees to the doctrine of the Church which must be held by all the faithful. Among these opinions it noted especially, as of greater importance, those which pertain to the dogma of faith about infallibility in the Church, to the task of authentically interpreting the unique sacred deposit of the word of

God which has been entrusted only to the living *Magisterium* of the Church, and finally to the valid consecration of the Eucharist.

At the same time this Sacred Congregation warned Professor Küng that he should not continue to teach such opinions, expecting in the meantime that he would bring his opinions into harmony with the doctrine of the authentic *Magisterium*.[8]

However, up to the present time he has in no way changed his opinion on the matters called to his attention.

This fact is particularly evident in the matter of the opinion which at least puts in doubt the dogma of infallibility in the Church or reduces it to a certain fundamental indefectibility of the Church in truth, with the possibility of error in doctrinal statements which the *Magisterium* of the Church teaches must be held definitively. On this point Hans Küng has in no way sought to conform to the doctrine of the *Magisterium*. Instead he has recently proposed his view again more explicitly (namely, in his writings, *Kirche – Gehalten in der Wahrheit?* – Benziger Verlag, 1979 – and *Zum Geleit*, an introduction to the work of A. B. Hasler entitled *Wie der Papst unfehlbar wurde* – Piper Verlag, 1979), even though this Sacred Congregation had affirmed that such an opinion contradicts the doctrine defined by Vatican Council I and confirmed by Vatican Council II.

Moreover, the consequences of this opinion, especially a contempt for the *Magisterium* of the Church, may be found in other works published by him, undoubtedly with serious harm to some essential points of Catholic faith (e.g., those teachings which pertain to the consubstantiality of Christ with his Father, and to the Blessed Virgin Mary), since the meaning ascribed to these doctrines is different from that which the Church has understood and now understands.

The Sacred Congregation for the Doctrine of Faith in the aforesaid document of 1975 refrained at the time from further action regarding the above-mentioned opinions of Professor Küng, presuming that he himself would abandon them. But since this presumption no longer exists, this Sacred Congregation by reason of its duty is constrained to declare that Professor Hans Küng, in his writings, has departed from the integral truth of Catholic faith, and therefore he can no longer be considered a Catholic theologian nor function as such in a teaching role.

At an audience granted to the under-signed Cardinal Prefect, the Supreme Pontiff Pope John Paul II approved this Declaration, decided upon at an Ordinary Meeting of this Sacred Congregation, and ordered its publication

In Rome, at the Sacred Congregation for the Doctrine of Faith, on 18 December 1979.

Franjo Cardinal Seper
Prefect

+ Fr Jérôme Hamer O.P.
Titular Archbishop of Lorium
Secretary

END NOTES

1. Cf. Conc. Vatic. I, Const. dogm. *Dei Filius*, cap. IV 'De fide et Ratione': DS 3018; Conc. Vatic. II, Const. dogm. *Lumen Gentium*, n. 12.
2. Cf. Conc. Vatic. II, Const. dogm. *Dei verbum*, n. 10.
3. Paulus VI, *Allocut. ad Congress. Internat. de Theologia Conc. Vatic. II*, 1 October 1966; A.A.S. 58 (1966), p. 891.
4. Cf. Ioannes Paulus II, Const. apost. *Sapientia christiana*, art. 70; Encycl. *Redemptor hominis*, n. 19; A.A.S. 71 (1979), pp. 493; 308.
5. Cf. Conc. Vatic. II, Const. dogm. *Lumen Gentium*, n. 11 and 25; Paulus VI Adhort. apost. *Quinque iam anni*: A.A.S. 63 (1971), p. 99f.
6. Cf. *Sapientia christiana*, tit. III, art. 27, par. 1: A.A.S. 71 (1979), p. 483.
7. Cf. *Motu proprio: Integrae servandae*, n. 1, 3 and 4: A.A.S. 57 (1965), p. 954.
8. Cf. A.A.S. 67 (1975), pp. 203–4.

Appendix 3. *Declaration of the German Bishops Conference*

'1) In a declaration dated 15 December 1979, the Congregation for the Doctrine of Faith stated: "In his writings, Professor Küng deviates from the complete truth of the Catholic belief. For this reason he cannot be regarded as a Catholic theologian as such. Accordingly the competent diocesan bishop, Mgr Georg Moser, will inform the science minister of the federal *Land* of Baden-Württemberg that the conditions for the *nihil obstat* are no longer fulfilled, and that Professor Küng will be deprived of the *missio canonica* accorded to him at his nomination to the University of Tübingen 19 years ago." Thus the unavoidable consequences have been drawn after nearly ten years of efforts to clarify theological fundamentals that are doubted by Professor Küng. The German Bishops' Conference regrets the need for this painful decision. It absolutely supports the decision of the Congregation for the Doctrine of Faith and the resulting measures of Bishop Moser. Considering the overall development there was no other way out.

'2) The main reason for the congregation's decision lies in Professor Küng's teaching about infallibility in the Church. All Christian churches and communities teach the indestructibility of the Church of Jesus Christ, which is mainly based on the undeviating strength and the firm certainty of the Word of God. Although the Church's belief has constantly to be rethought and this process will remain uncompleted until the end of history, it includes a binding "yes" and an unequivocal "no". Otherwise it is not possible for the Church to stay in the truth. Furthermore, the Catholic Church is convinced that the Church as a whole and in its own special way its ministry (episcopate, council, pope) is endowed with the Holy Spirit's gift to preserve and to interpret unmistakably the once-given Word of God in the strength of its particular truth.

Therefore certain statements of faith are part of the Church's hold on the truth. These have a different degree of binding power. Statements of faith which serve to interpret the Scriptures and are expressed with ultimate binding force by the Church are "dogma" in the power sense. Vatican I dogmatized the infallibility of pronouncements by the Pope and at the same time described the conditions for that kind of authoritative speaking emerging from the tradition of the Church. Vatican II has complemented and confirmed this doctrine.

'In his book *Unfehlbar? − Eine Anfrange*, as well as in other writings, Professor Küng limited this doctrine when he expressed his belief that the Church's basic hold on the truth is nevertheless compatible with factual errors in those decisions of faith which the Church's ministry has declared to be irreversible, the Church's hold on truth remaining, "despite possible errors". The CDF regards this as a reduction of the Church's endowment of infallibility and a radical obscuring of the dogma of 1870. Lately Professor Küng even took up the idea of a "revision of the decisions of Vatican I".

'The dogma of infallibility in the Church may at first be regarded as a phenomenon marginal to the whole corpus of the faith, but in reality it includes fundamental problems such as the knowledge of truth, interpretation of revelation, its linguistic form and its tradition, the certainty of faith, and the justification for the official authority of the Church. Errors in this domain, which serves true knowledge of divine revelation, are prejudicial to faith.

'The theological method followed by Professor Küng − its dangerous narrowness has often been pointed out − leads to a break on important matters with the Catholic tradition of faith and teaching. This becomes obvious mainly in Professor Küng's statements about the person of Jesus Christ. In the central question of christology, whether Jesus Christ is really God's Son, i.e. whether Jesus holds undiminished the position and state of being God, Professor Küng has evaded a decisive and binding confession, despite all efforts to clear this up. From the earliest

159

times, Christians confess: "We believe ... in the Lord, Jesus Christ, the only son of God, eternally begotten of the Father, God from God, light from light, true God from true God, begotten not made, one being with the Father" (thus the Nicene Creed, 325). This brings about consequences for our salvation: if God did not offer himself for the people in the person of Jesus Christ, then the vital part of the Christian revelation perishes. All pronouncements, even on the human nature of Jesus, are of real significance for Christian belief only when intimately related to the truth of his divinity.

'Professor Küng, indeed, generally affirms that he wants to preserve and to enhance the fundamental elements of Christological dogma. Nevertheless, he in fact obscures and reduces what they clearly say. Fundamental lack of clarity about the mystery of the person of Jesus Christ not only threatens the core of Catholic belief, but also Catholic belief in general.

'These insufficiencies have contributed to a worrying insecurity in belief. But even today the faithful have the right to a complete and clear presentation of the truths of faith. The Church has to take care of this in its teaching and pastoral ministry.'

*

The bishops then record in detail the exchanges that have taken place between the CDF and Professor Küng since 1967, when his book *Die Kirche* was first published in German. In April 1968 he agreed to take part in a colloquy on the subject, but this never took place. The publication of *Infallible?* in 1970 occasioned a 'voluminous correspondence' but no answer satisfying to the CDF, which 'entrusted with the protection and promotion of the faith of the whole Church', published, in July 1973, the declaration *Mysterium Ecclesiae* in which Professor Küng's teaching was specifically rejected. Once again a colloquy was suggested, and although this did not take place 'Küng assured the CDF by letter of his intention to make use of the "time for reflection" granted him and of the possibility that his "doctrine" might in the course of time "assimilate" to the official teaching'; the CDF declared its proceedings in this affair 'completed for the time being', though the German bishops, in an accompanying declaration, 17 February 1975, reminded Professor Küng 'of principles belonging to the basic understanding of Catholic theology which have not been sufficiently safeguarded in some of his writings'. Efforts to get 'amplification from Professor Küng' with regard to *On Being A Christian* failed in 1977, as they did also in 1978 with regard to his latest book, *Does God Exist?* Finally, despite the 1975 declaration 'Professor Küng, in spring 1979, not only repeated his doctrine about infallibility in the Church but expressed it even more sharply' notably in the preface to A. B. Hasler's recent book on infallibility (see *The Tablet*, 1 December).

*

'4) The decision that has been taken can only be understood in the light of almost ten years of discussion and controversy. The representatives of the CDF in Rome, the presidents of the German Bishops' Conference and its commission of faith, especially Cardinal Julius Döpfner and Cardinal Hermann Volk, as well as Bishop Georg Moser of Rottenburg-Stuttgart, in many letters, in personal conversations and in many initiatives tried to clear the situation up. They thereby conferred an important role on this theological dialogue. During these ten years Professor Küng has neither accepted the repeated invitations of the CDF, nor has he answered adequately the questions addressed to him by it and by the German Bishops' Conference. The temporary stay of the proceedings on doctrinal matters and the administering of the exhortation in 1975 represented a substantial concession and a new attempt to resolve the conflict. In an attitude of unparalleled intransigence and rare unconvincibility – despite affirmations of readiness for dialogue – he was not willing to change his mind as a result either of extended theological discussion or of the initiatives of the Church authorities for an amplification, modification or revision of his doctrines. His sometimes unrestrained attacks on the Church's discipline and order come into the same context.

'5) For this reason the decision taken by the CDF has become unavoidable. The German Bishops' Conference regrets the failure of so many efforts to find another solution. During recent years the Church has been blamed for tolerating such divergent teaching while taking a strong line, for example, towards Archbishop Lefebvre and his adherents.

'The CDF and the German Bishops' Conference, as well as the Bishop of Rottenburg, have left no room for doubt that they will not ignore their duty to protect the belief of the Church. The members of the Church for their part have the right to an authentic preaching of and certainty in the faith (not to be confused with false security!) which are made possible by the doctrinal authority of the Church and therefore also by the infallibility given by the Spirit of God. Commitment to this conviction means maintenance of the identity of the Catholic Church, which is a condition for real ecumenical dialogue and the fulfilment of the Church's tasks in society.

'The German Bishops' Conference asks the faithful of the Catholic Church and other Christians and all people who are interested in the life of the Church, to see and judge the decision of the CDF against this background. The Church's ministry will not allow itself to be deterred by this disappointing event from searching, even in the future, for a solution to clear up controversial theological opinions with the help of open dialogue.

'6) By the withdrawal of his canonical commission, Professor Küng loses his licence to teach Catholic theology in the name of the Church. He is not excluded from the Church and remains a priest.'

Cologne, 18 December 1979
> Joseph Cardinal Höffner, President of the German
> Bishops' Conference

Appendix 4. *Hans Küng's 'Appeal'*
Statement

I have always considered myself to be a Catholic theologian and I will continue to do so. Today as before I consider myself to be a priest of the *ecclesia Catholica*. As a Catholic theologian I had and have a special concern for the 'Catholic Church', that is the 'general, the all-embracing, the universal Church'. For that reason I have tried and try to teach Christian truth in all its Catholic breadth and depth. So all my life I have been concerned with the unbroken continuity – through whatever ruptures of faith and the community of faith: that is 'catholicity' *in time*. Likewise I have stressed the universality of faith and of the believing community which unites different groups: that is 'catholicity' *in space*. In this spirit I would like to continue to represent Catholic teaching as a Catholic theologian. I know that in this I am at one with countless theologians, pastors, teachers of religion and lay people.

On the most recent Declaration of the Congregation for the Doctrine of Faith I would like to make the following remarks, beginning with some general points.

In my most recent publications on infallibility there is no question of any sharpening of earlier views – still less of any 'contumacy' – but rather of a constructive clarification of what is at issue in the debate on infallibility. In my introduction to Hasler's book I simply gathered together some of the thoughts in my 'Survey' of the infallibility discussion published in 1973, adding a report on its results. In the short meditation, *The Church – Maintained in the Truth?*, written at the same time, one reads explicitly: 'This meditation is not designed to provoke a fresh controversy on infallibility.' My concern was not and is not with an attack but with a question; and I am ready to have my ideas tested in a new investigation. For that reason both in my introduction to Hasler and in the meditation, and following up the suggestion of the French theologian Yves Congar, Rome was invited to set up an ecumenical commission of experts to consider the question.

It was certainly not any 'contempt for the *magisterium* of the Church' (this charge I must reject vigorously) but rather a concern to give a new credibility to the teaching authority in the Church and in the world that inspired my theological work to date. And in no way have I set up 'my own judgement as the norm of truth' – still less in contrast to the faith of the Church; instead, with scholarly integrity and loyalty to the Church, my whole theological work has been directed to the Gospel of Jesus Christ and the Catholic tradition.

I cannot of course conceal that I had certain criticisms of the procedure of the Congregation for the Doctrine of Faith. It makes no sense to me that the CDF, before taking this most recent and grievous step, should not have given me the chance to speak and justify my positions. It is also unacceptable that the CDF should have raised grave objections against my ideas on 'some essential points of Catholic faith (Christology, mariology)', although these matters were never part of a Roman procedure against me.

After these general considerations, a few remarks on the central issue: my conception of the *magisterium* and of infallibility is one-sidedly and negatively understood by the CDF. As a clarification, I would like to make the following remarks – which follow from the statement of the German bishops of 4 March 1971.

In my previous writings on infallibility I have never questioned the following points: there are certain Church statements that are true and recognizably true; their meaning remains the same despite the historical changes in modes of thought, and they require an unambiguous yes or no.

Likewise I acknowledge that the Church has the duty and the task of preaching the Christian message in relation to the Gospel and of expressing it clearly and bindingly. Of course at the same time one has to take seriously the Declaration *Mysterium Ecclesiae* (1973) on the historical conditioning of all dogmatic statements.

I have also always agreed that bishops are entrusted in a special way with the responsibility for the Church's remaining in the truth, and that in certain circumstances they need to express Christian truth in binding terms against whatever is unChristian (definitions of faith or dogmas). In this regard ecumenical councils, as a representation of the whole Church together with the Bishop of Rome as its head, have a special authority. I have always given special importance to ecumenical councils, and precisely on the question of christology have based myself on the ancient councils of the Church and tried to make their teaching intelligible for our contemporaries.

As for the First Vatican Council, it was never my intention to deny its definitions of faith or to question the Petrine office, still less to make my own opinion the measure of Catholic faith or to disturb the Catholic people in their faith. On the contrary! This is a real and genuine question, and the continuing international debate had at least one result: very many theologians, whose catholicism is not at all in doubt, admitted the necessity and legitimacy of raising this question.

I beg earnestly that I should be believed when I say – knowing perfectly well the personal risk that I am running – that I wanted to provide a service for our Church, so that this question which is burdensome for so many within and without the Church might be clarified in a spirit of Christian responsibility. This question is of importance precisely for an understanding with the Orthodox Churches, to which Pope John Paul II has given new and hope-filled impetus by setting up a special commission. Ecumenical considerations also demand a further discussion of the matter. This statement is sustained by the confidence that the present conflict – with all its unpredictable consequences – could be resolved positively in a spirit of genuine catholicity.

Tübingen   Hans Küng

Appendix 5. *Declaration of the Holy See,* 30 December 1979

1) The Declaration of the Congregation for the Doctrine of Faith (15 December 1979) on some points in the theological doctrine of Professor Küng was intended to protect the right of the faithful to receive the integral truth taught by the Church. All the previous efforts of the Holy See, the German Bishops' Conference and the local Bishop to help Professor Küng to overcome his erroneous conceptions, were without success.

2) In conversation with Bishop Moser Professor Küng had declared his readiness to clarify his doctrinal ideas still further; and on this basis Bishop Moser, with great patience and personal friendliness towards Professor Küng, tried to help towards a solution of the problem. The Holy Father was informed that Professor Küng, after his meetings with Bishop Moser, had signed a statement. The Holy Father then decided to invite the German cardinals, Bishop Moser and the Metropolitan Archbishop of Freiburg-im-Bresgau to a special consultation, at which the Cardinal Secretary of State and the Prefect and Secretary of the Congregation for the Doctrine of Faith were also present.

After a thorough examination of the latest remarks of Professor Küng, all the participants in the consultation reached the conclusion that unfortunately these did not provide sufficient grounds to alter the decision laid down in the 15 December Declaration.

3) Consequently Professor Küng cannot continue in a teaching post which depends upon the Church. The appropriate Ordinary is therefore bound to draw the necessary conclusions in accordance with canon law and the Concordat.

4) The Congregation for the Doctrine of Faith has for years striven to get Professor Küng to clarify the ideas he had so widely diffused, but without finding any corre-

sponding willingness to talk on his side. The 28 December consultation is a further proof that the Holy See and the German bishops have handled the problem of Professor Küng with great good will.

The decision that had to be regretfully taken after so many previous efforts is motivated exclusively by a deep sense of pastoral responsibility.

It does not in the slightest mean – as the 15 December Declaration already stated – any limitation on the legitimate and necessary freedom of theological research.

Nor does the decision change the attitude of the Church in its striving towards Christian unity according to the principles of the Declaration of Vatican II, *Unitatis Redintegratio.*

5) Although Professor Küng's statement does not provide a sufficient basis to change the decision contained in the 15 December Declaration, the Holy See and the German bishops have not given up hope that Professor Küng – who has often declared his intention of remaining a Catholic theologian – will after deeper reflection adopt an attitude that would permit his permission to teach to be restored.

The Holy See and the German bishops will recommend this matter to the Lord in prayer, and invite all men of good will to join with them.

BOOKS QUOTED

Abbott, Walter, S.J., and Gallagher, Joseph, eds., *The Documents of Vatican II*, Geoffrey Chapman, London, and America Press, New York, 1966

Auwerda, Richard, *Dossier Schillebeeckx. Theolog in de Kerk der conflicten*, Nelissen, Bilthoven, 1969

Brown, Raymond E., *Biblical Reflections on Crises Facing the Church*, Darton, Longman and Todd, London, and Paulist Press, New York, 1975

Dulles, Avery, S.J., *The Resilient Church*, Gill and Macmillan, Dublin, and Doubleday, New York, 1978

Galot, Jean, S.J., *Cristo Contestato*, Libreria Editrice Fiorentina, 1979

Hamer, Jérôme, O.P., *The Church is a Communion*, English translation Geoffrey Chapman, London, and New York, 1964

Hebblethwaite, Peter, *The Runaway Church*, Collins, London, and Seabury Press, New York, 1975
The Year of Three Popes, Collins and Fount Paperbacks, London and Cleveland, 1978

Küng, Hans, *The Living Church*, Sheed & Ward, London, and (US title: *The Council in Action*) New York, 1963
The Church, Burns & Oates, London, and Sheed & Ward, New York, 1967
Infallible? An Enquiry, Collins, London, and Doubleday, New York, 1971. Paperback: Fontana, London, and Image Books, New York, 1972
Does God Exist?, Collins, London and Doubleday, New York, 1980 (due late in year)

Mackey, James P., *Jesus, the Man and the Myth*, S.C.M. Press, London and Paulist Press, New York, 1979

Malinski, Mieczyslaw, *Pope John Paul: The Life of My Friend Karol Wojtyla*, Burns & Oates, London, and Seabury Press, New York, 1979

O'Collins, Gerald, S.J., *What are they Saying about Jesus?*, Paulist Press, New York, 1977

Oram, James, *The People's Pope*, Bay Books, Sydney and London, and Chronicle Books, San Francisco, 1979

Pohier, Jacques, O.P., *Quand je dis Dieu*, 1977; Eng. trans. *When I Say God*, Seabury Press, New York, 1980

Schillebeeckx, Edward, *Christ the Sacrament*, Sheed & Ward, London and New York, 1963
The Eucharist, Sheed & Ward, London and New York, 1968
Jesus – An Experiment in Christology, Collins, London, and Seabury Press, New York, 1979

Wojtyla, Karol (Pope John Paul II), *The Acting Person*, D. Reidel, Dordrecht, Holland, 1979
Love and Responsibility, Collins, London, and Farrar, Straus & Giroux, New York, 1980 (due late in year)
Sign of Contradiction, St Paul Publications, London, and Seabury Press, New York, 1979

INDEX OF NAMES

ABOUT THE AUTHOR

Near Manchester in 1930, Peter Hebblethwaite set out. College course of Jesuit training at the age of seventeen. became a philosophy in France, picked up a first in Jesuit assistant languages at Oxford (where he was reported periodical *The* in a rural setting. In 1965 he and studied theology at Heythrop Roman synods, and the other major ecclesiastical subsequent the decade, as well as the tentative beginnings of Christian-Marxist dialogue. this vantage-point he afterwards editor of the final session of

In January 1974 he resigned from the Jesuits, while maintaining good relations with them, and began to work as a free-lance writer. He reported on the two conclaves of 1978 for *The Sunday Times*, and since September 1979 has been living in Rome as the Vatican Affairs correspondent of the (American) *National Catholic Reporter* and his account of the two conclaves of 1978, *The Year of Three Popes*. He is also a contributor to *The Runaway Church* and his account of and Fount, 1980), and translator of *The Pope from Poland: An Assessment* (Collins *Cosmas, or The Love of God* (Collins, 1980).

GAYLORD

PRINTED IN U.S.A.

ABOUT THE AUTHOR

Born near Manchester in 1930, Peter Hebblethwaite set out on the long course of Jesuit training at the age of seventeen. He delved into philosophy in France, picked up a first in medieval and modern languages at Oxford (where he was later to teach them), and studied theology at Heythrop College when it was still in a rural setting. In 1965 he became assistant editor and shortly afterwards editor of the Jesuit periodical *The Month*. From this vantage-point he reported the final session of the Vatican Council, subsequent Roman synods, and the other major ecclesiastical events of the decade, as well as the tentative beginnings of Christian-Marxist dialogue.

In January 1974 he resigned from the Jesuits, while maintaining good relations with them, and began to work as a free-lance writer. He reported on the two conclaves of 1978 for *The Sunday Times*, and since September 1979 has been living in Rome as the Vatican Affairs correspondent of the (American) *National Catholic Reporter*

His books include *The Runaway Church* and his account of the two conclaves of 1978, *The Year of Three Popes*. He is also a contributor to *The Pope from Poland: An Assessment* (Collins and Fount, 1980), and translator of *Cosmas, or The Love of God* (Collins, 1980).